Chinese Character Practice Workbook

FOR KIDS

100 Essential Chinese Characters MADE EASY

RACHEL AVRICK, MA

ILLUSTRATION BY REMIE GEOFFROI

callisto
publishing
an imprint of Sourcebooks

Published by Callisto Publishing LLC C/O Sourcebooks LLC
P.O. Box 4410, Naperville, Illinois 60567-4410
(630) 961-3900
callistopublishing.com

Printed in the United States of America.

This Book Belongs to:

Contents

100 CHARACTERS LIST v
LET'S GET STARTED vi

One *Yī* 1
Two *Èr* 2
Three *Sān* 3
Four *Sì* 4
Five *Wǔ* 5
Six *Liù* 6
Seven *Qī* 7
Eight *Bā* 8
Nine *Jiǔ* 9
Ten *Shí* 10
Person *Rén* 11
Enter *Rù* 12
Strength *Lì* 13
Knife *Dāo* 14
Big *Dà* 15
Small *Xiǎo* 16
Sunset/Evening *Xī* 17
Mountain *Shān* 18
River *Chuān* 19
Ground/Soil *Tǔ* 20
Door *Mén* 21
Work *Gōng* 22
Mouth *Kǒu* 23
Horse *Mǎ* 24
Child *Zǐ* 25
Female/Woman *Nǚ* 26
Fly *Fēi* 27
Measure Word *Gè* 28
Up *Shàng* 29
Down *Xià* 30
Moon/Month *Yuè* 31
Sun/Day *Rì* 32
Tree/Wood *Mù* 33
Water *Shuǐ* 34

Sky *Tiān* 35
Fire *Huǒ* 36
Wind *Fēng* 37
Air *Qì* 38
Cloud *Yún* 39
Cow *Niú* 40
Heart *Xīn* 41
Tooth *Yá* 42
Hand *Shǒu* 43
Father *Fù* 44
King *Wáng* 45
Friend *Yǒu* 46
Book *Shū* 47
Open *Kāi* 48
Grow *Zhǎng* 49
Middle *Zhōng* 50
Car *Chē* 51
No/Not *Bù* 52
White *Bái* 53
Field *Tián* 54
Grain *Hé* 55
Leaf *Yè* 56
Winter *Dōng* 57
Bird *Niǎo* 58
Dragon *Lóng* 59
Left *Zuǒ* 60
Right *Yòu* 61
Head *Tóu* 62
Eye *Mù* 63
Birth *Shēng* 64
Bag/Package *Bāo* 65
Write *Xiě* 66
Go *Qù* 67
Prisoner *Qiú* 68

He/Him *Tā* 69
Happy *Lè* 70
Use *Yòng* 71
Correct *Duì* 72
Hundred *Bǎi* 73
Red *Hóng* 74
Color *Sè* 75
Rice *Mǐ* 76
Earth/Ground *Dì* 77
Bamboo *Zhú* 78
Morning *Zǎo* 79
Sheep *Yáng* 80
Ear *Ěr* 81
Worm *Chóng* 82
Mom *Mā* 83
She/Her *Tā* 84
Close *Guān* 85
Eat *Chī* 86
Name *Míng* 87
Clothes *Yī* 88
Umbrella *Sǎn* 89
Good *Hǎo* 90
Ask *Wèn* 91
Male/Man *Nán* 92
Chicken *Jī* 93
Listen *Tīng* 94
Bright *Míng* 95
Woods *Lín* 96
Rain *Yǔ* 97
Fish *Yú* 98
Friend *Péng* 99
Study/Learn *Xué* 100

MORE PRACTICE SPACE 101   COMMON CHINESE PHRASES 112   RESOURCES 113

100 Characters List

一 *Yī* One	二 *Èr* Two	三 *Sān* Three	四 *Sì* Four	五 *Wǔ* Five	六 *Liù* Six	七 *Qī* Seven	八 *Bā* Eight	九 *Jiǔ* Nine	十 *Shí* Ten
人 *Rén* Person	入 *Rù* Enter	力 *Lì* Strength	刀 *Dāo* Knife	大 *Dà* Big	小 *Xiǎo* Small	夕 *Xī* Sunset/Evening	山 *Shān* Mountain	川 *Chuān* River	土 *Tǔ* Ground/Soil
门 *Mén* Door	工 *Gōng* Work	口 *Kǒu* Mouth	马 *Mǎ* Horse	子 *Zǐ* Child	女 *Nǚ* Female/Woman	飞 *Fēi* Fly	个 *Gè* Measure Word	上 *Shàng* Up	下 *Xià* Down
月 *Yuè* Moon/Month	日 *Rì* Sun/Day	木 *Mù* Tree/Wood	水 *Shuǐ* Water	天 *Tiān* Sky	火 *Huǒ* Fire	风 *Fēng* Wind	气 *Qì* Air	云 *Yún* Cloud	牛 *Niú* Cow
心 *Xīn* Heart	牙 *Yá* Tooth	手 *Shǒu* Hand	父 *Fù* Father	王 *Wáng* King	友 *Yǒu* Friend	书 *Shū* Book	开 *Kāi* Open	长 *Zhǎng* Grow	中 *Zhōng* Middle
车 *Chē* Car	不 *Bù* No/Not	白 *Bái* White	田 *Tián* Field	禾 *Hé* Grain	叶 *Yè* Leaf	冬 *Dōng* Winter	鸟 *Niǎo* Bird	龙 *Lóng* Dragon	左 *Zuǒ* Left
右 *Yòu* Right	头 *Tóu* Head	目 *Mù* Eye	生 *Shēng* Birth	包 *Bāo* Bag/Package	写 *Xiě* Write	去 *Qù* Go	囚 *Qiú* Prisoner	他 *Tā* He/Him	乐 *Lè* Happy
用 *Yòng* Use	对 *Duì* Correct	百 *Bǎi* Hundred	红 *Hóng* Red	色 *Sè* Color	米 *Mǐ* Rice	地 *Dì* Earth/Ground	竹 *Zhú* Bamboo	早 *Zǎo* Morning	羊 *Yáng* Sheep
耳 *Ěr* Ear	虫 *Chóng* Worm	妈 *Mā* Mom	她 *Tā* She/Her	关 *Guān* Close	吃 *Chī* Eat	名 *Míng* Name	衣 *Yī* Clothes	伞 *Sǎn* Umbrella	好 *Hǎo* Good
问 *Wèn* Ask	男 *Nán* Male/Man	鸡 *Jī* Chicken	听 *Tīng* Listen	明 *Míng* Bright	林 *Lín* Woods	雨 *Yǔ* Rain	鱼 *Yú* Fish	朋 *Péng* Friend	学 *Xué* Study/Learn

Let's Get Started

Hi! I'm so glad you're here. Did you know that Chinese uses symbols called characters instead of letters? In this workbook, you're going to have the chance to write some awesome Chinese characters.

There are 11 different categories of characters that you will learn to write. They are:

ABSTRACT	BODY	NUMBERS	THEMES
ADJECTIVES	COLOR	PEOPLE	VERBS
ANIMALS	NATURE	SCHOOL	

I chose these 100 characters because they are the building blocks of the Chinese language. Many of these characters are used to create bigger characters. Also, many of the 100 characters look like pictures of what they mean.

This book will help you see the correct order to write the strokes in each character. Chinese characters are mostly written from left to right, or top to bottom.

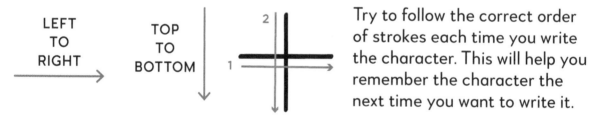

LEFT TO RIGHT

TOP TO BOTTOM

Try to follow the correct order of strokes each time you write the character. This will help you remember the character the next time you want to write it.

On each page, you will see the Chinese character to practice, as well as the "pinyin," or what the character sounds like when spoken. If you see a funny mark in the pinyin, like "mā," that shows you the direction your voice should go. There is plenty of room for you to practice on each page. There are extra practice pages in the back of the book, too!

There are two writing forms in Chinese. Traditional Chinese is used in Taiwan and Hong Kong and has more strokes in its characters. Simplified Chinese is used in mainland China and Singapore. These characters have fewer strokes. Not all traditional Chinese characters are simplified, but some are due to their complexity. This book uses both.

Take your time, do your best, and continue to practice these characters even after you complete this book. Let yourself have fun with it!

Character: 一
English: one
Strokes: 1
Pinyin: *yī*

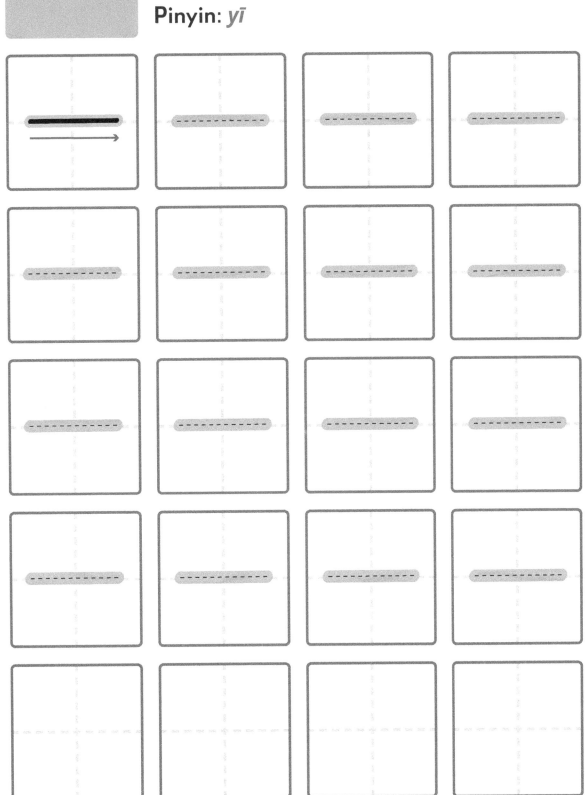

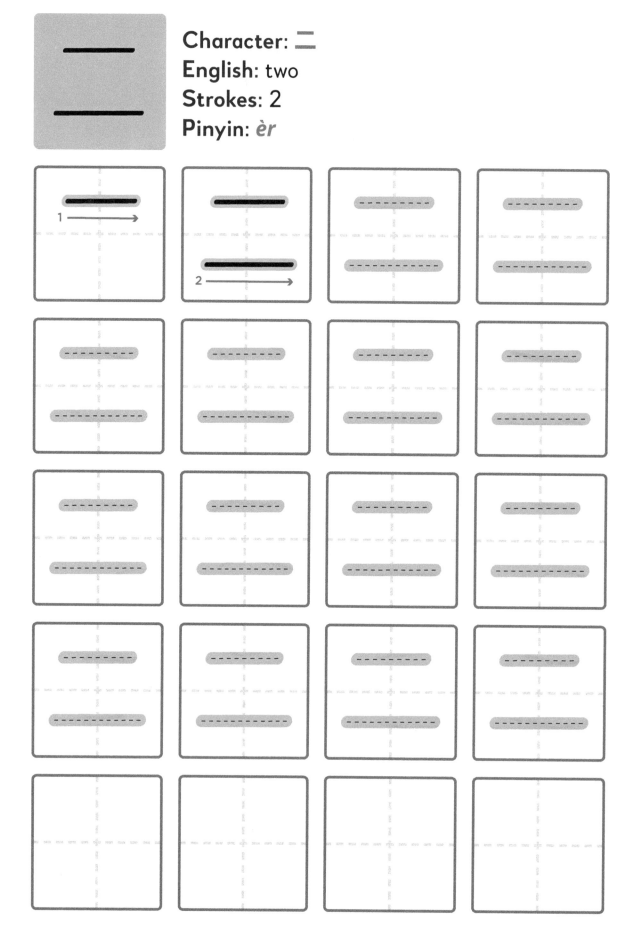

Character: 二
English: two
Strokes: 2
Pinyin: *èr*

Character: 三
English: three
Strokes: 3
Pinyin: *sān*

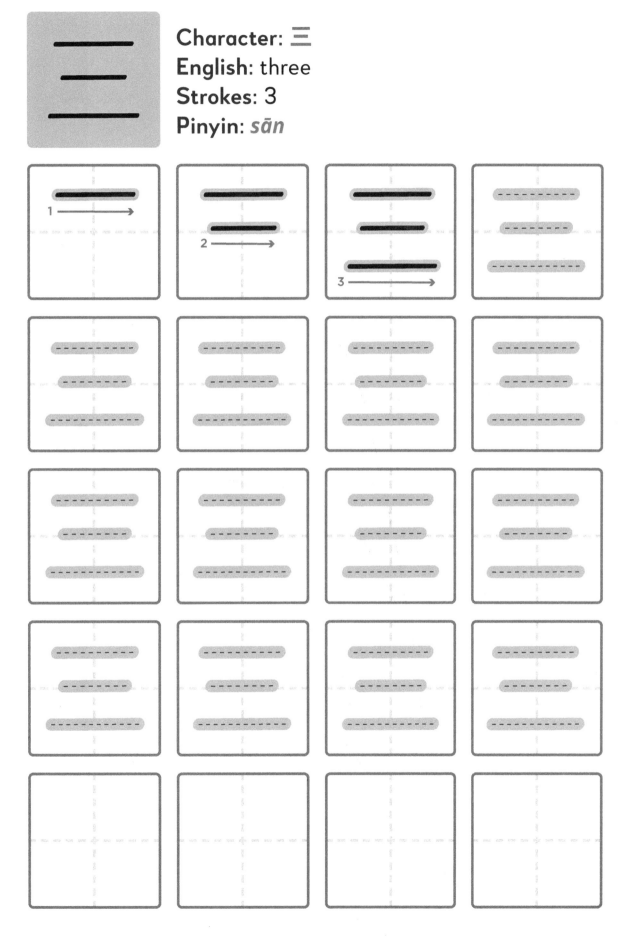

Character: 四
English: four
Strokes: 5
Pinyin: *sì*

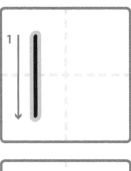
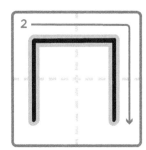
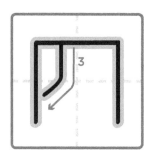
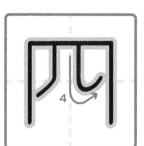

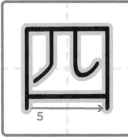
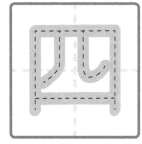

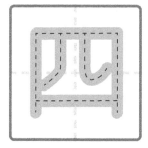

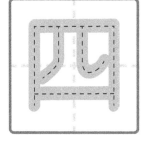
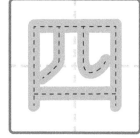
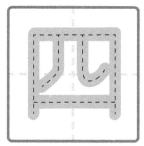

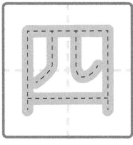
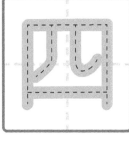
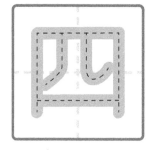
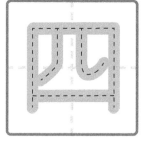

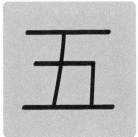

Character: 五
English: five
Strokes: 4
Pinyin: *wǔ*

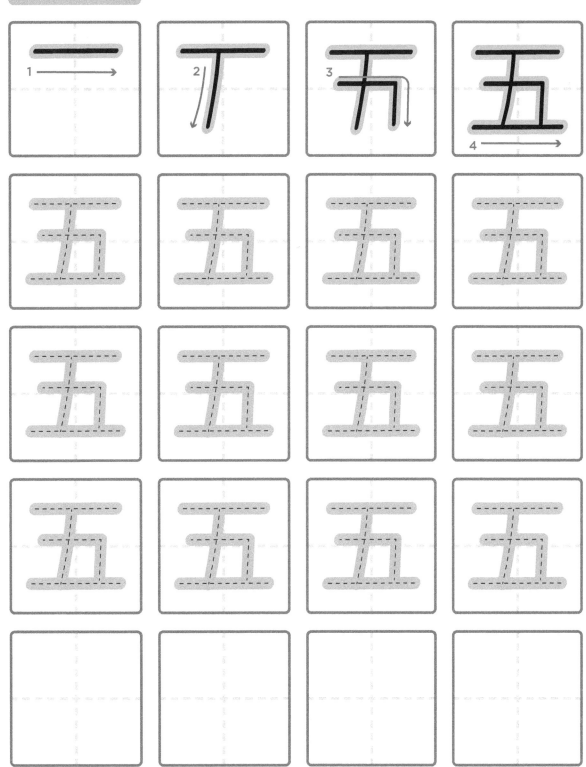

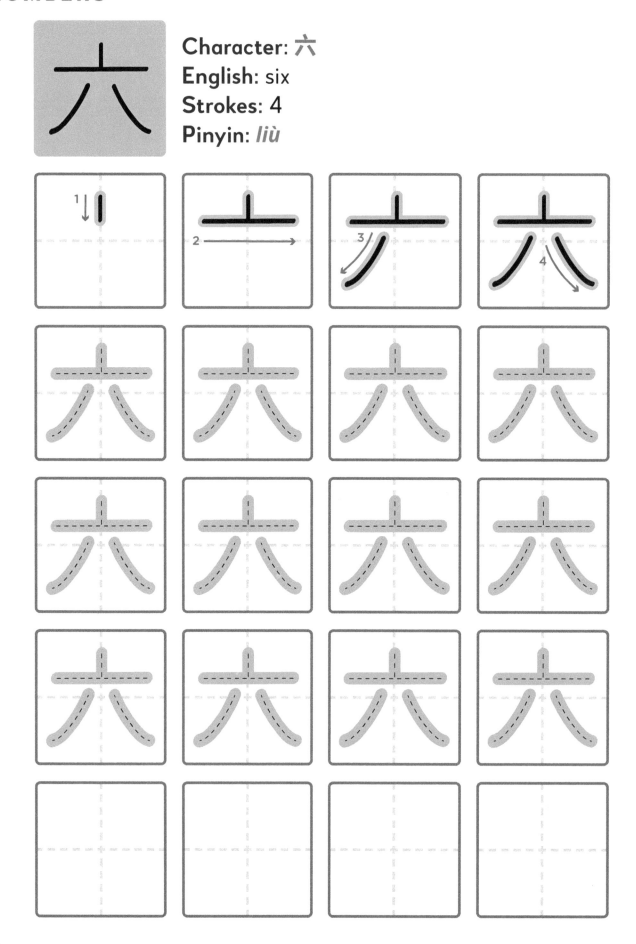

Character: 六
English: six
Strokes: 4
Pinyin: *liù*

CHINESE CHARACTER PRACTICE WORKBOOK FOR KIDS

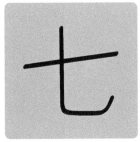

Character: 七
English: seven
Strokes: 2
Pinyin: *qī*

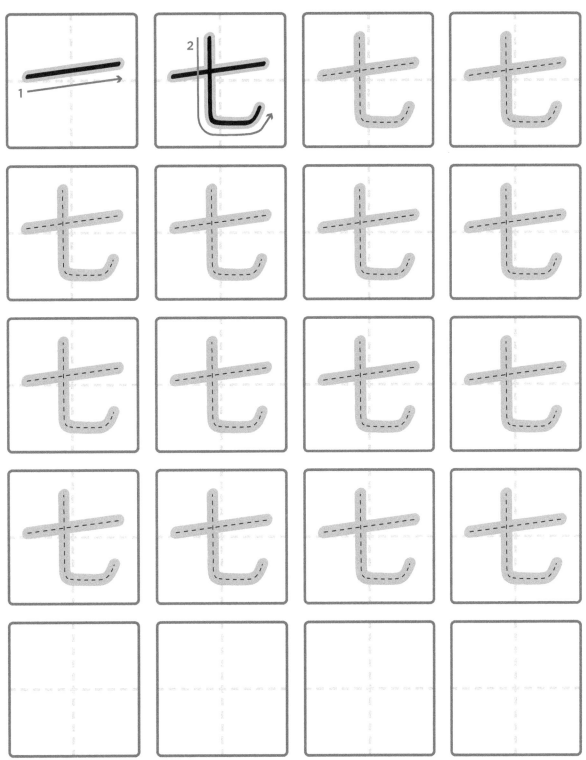

Character: 八
English: eight
Strokes: 2
Pinyin: *bā*

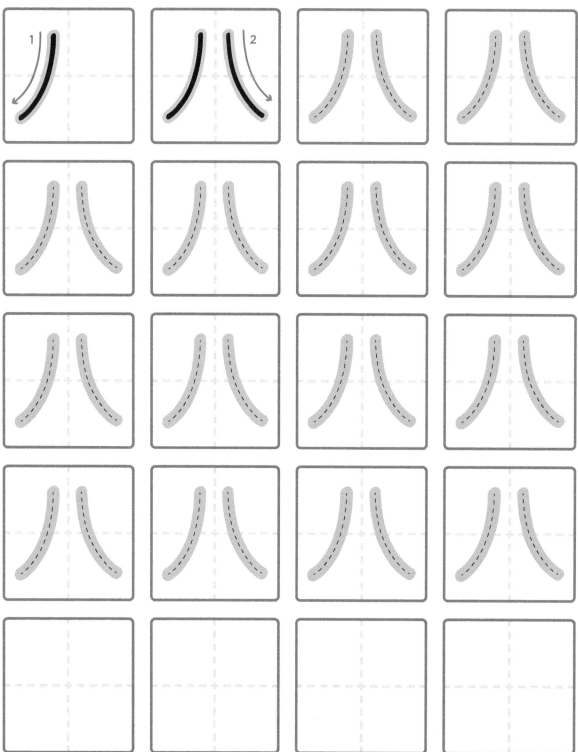

CHINESE CHARACTER PRACTICE WORKBOOK FOR KIDS

Character: 九
English: nine
Strokes: 2
Pinyin: *jiǔ*

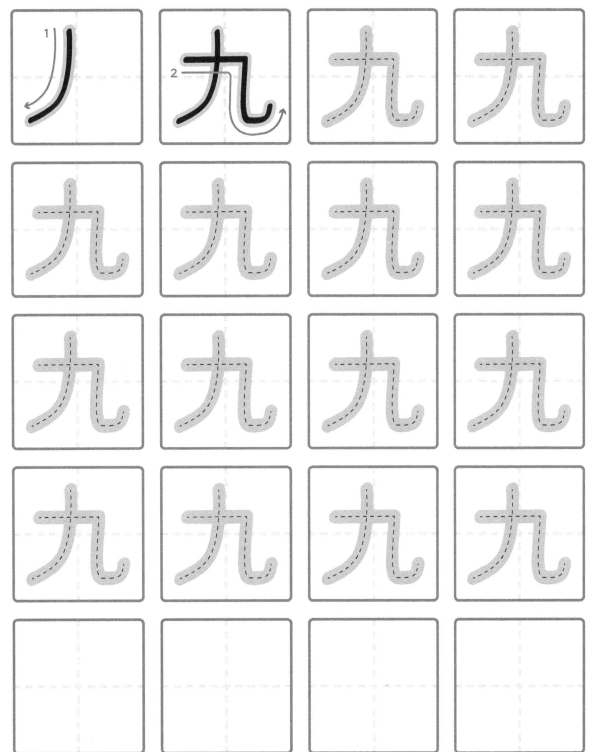

Character: 十
English: ten
Strokes: 2
Pinyin: *shí*

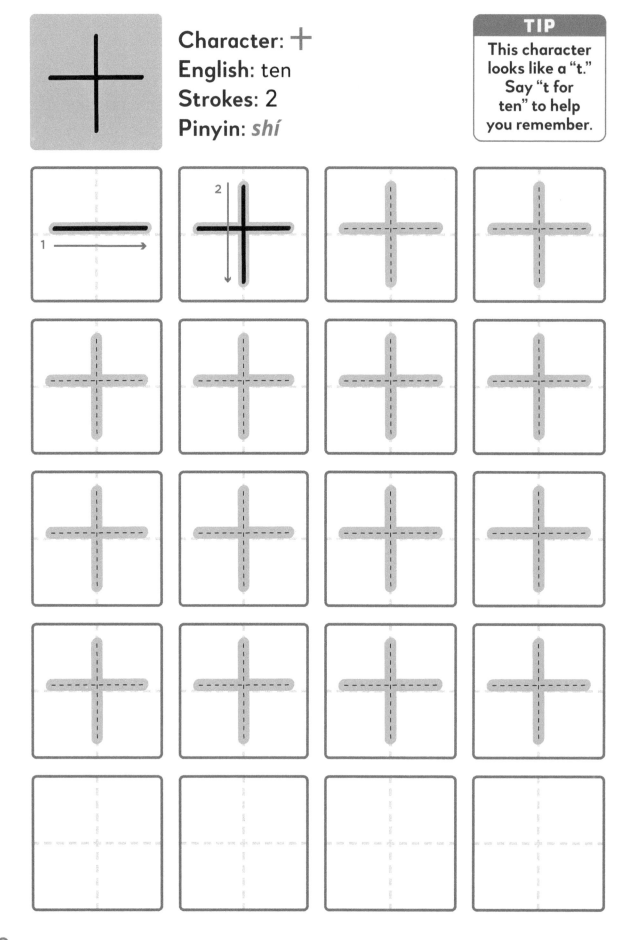

Character: 人
English: person
Strokes: 2
Pinyin: *rén*

TIP

An easy way to memorize this character is by remembering that a person walks with their legs.

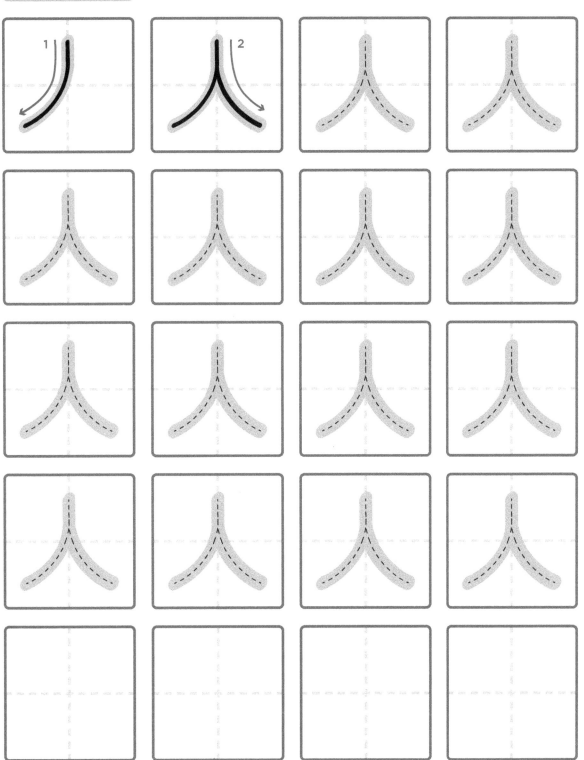

Character: 入
English: enter
Strokes: 2
Pinyin: *rù*

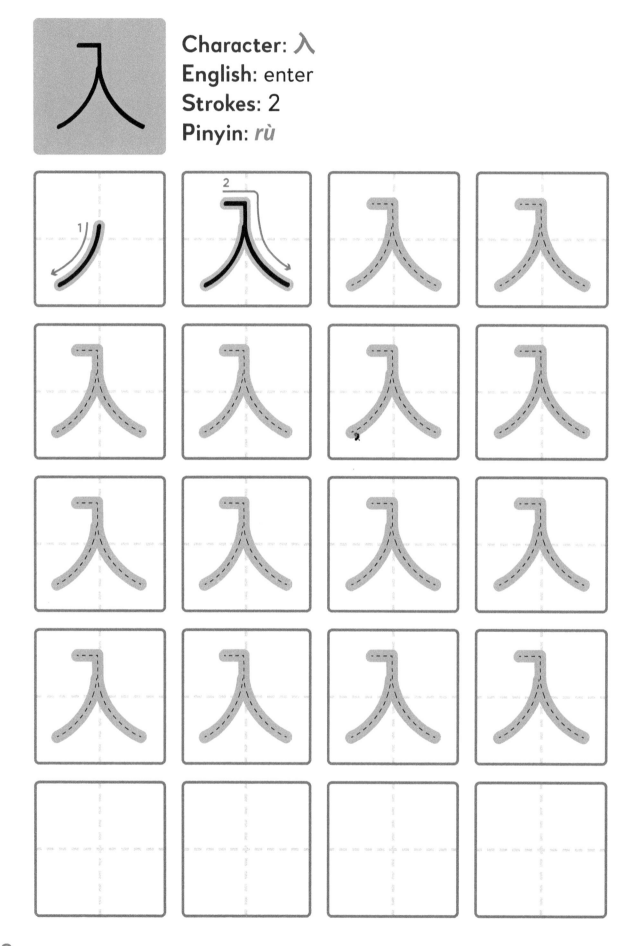

Character: 力
English: strength
Strokes: 2
Pinyin: *lì*

TIP
This character is the bottom half of the character for "male": 男. Check out page 92 for how to write this character!

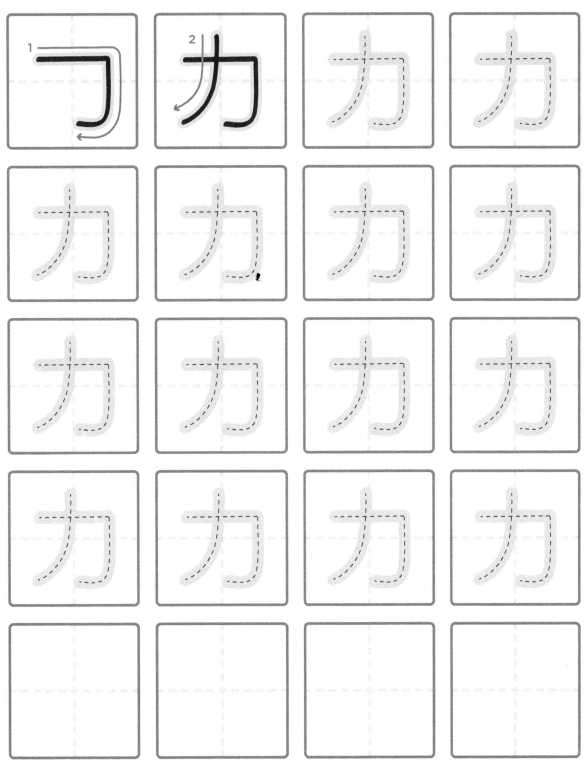

刀

Character: 刀
English: knife
Strokes: 2
Pinyin: *dāo*

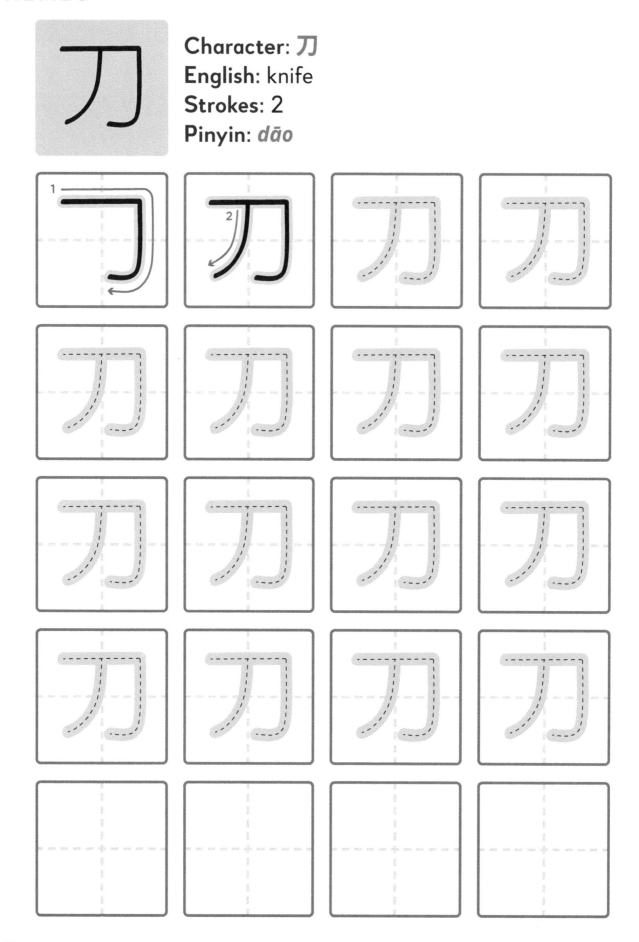

Character: 大
English: big
Strokes: 3
Pinyin: *dà*

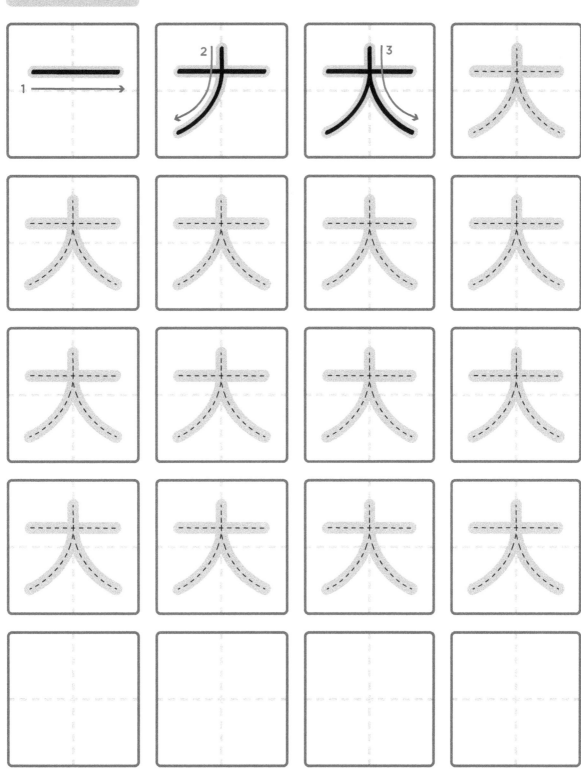

Character: 小
English: small
Strokes: 3
Pinyin: *xiǎo*

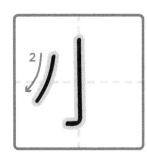 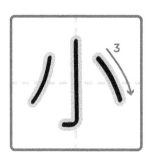 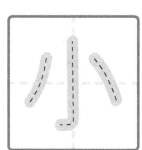 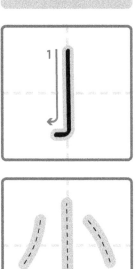

 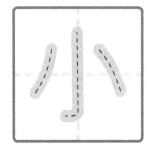 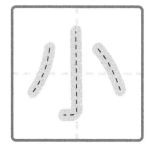 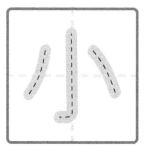

 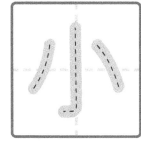 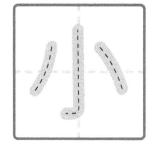 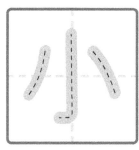

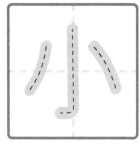 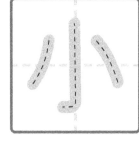 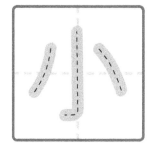 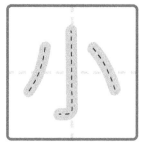

Character: 夕
English: sunset/evening
Strokes: 3
Pinyin: *xī*

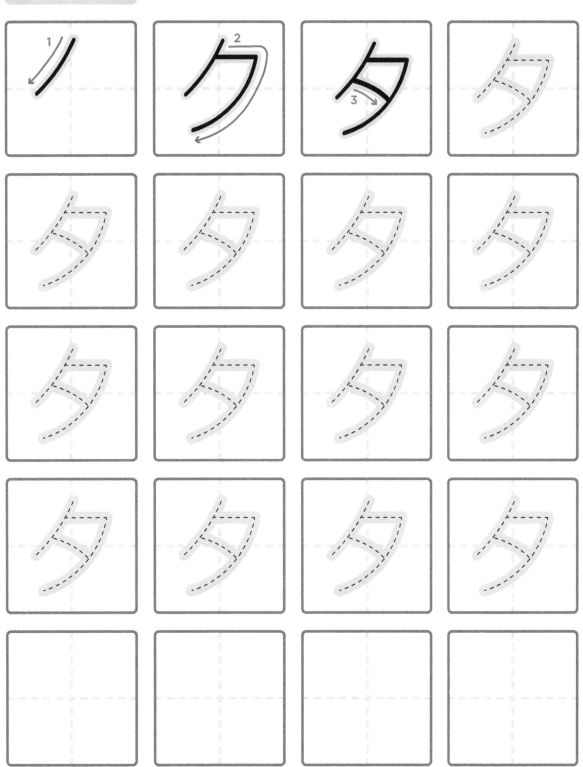

Character: 山
English: mountain
Strokes: 3
Pinyin: *shān*

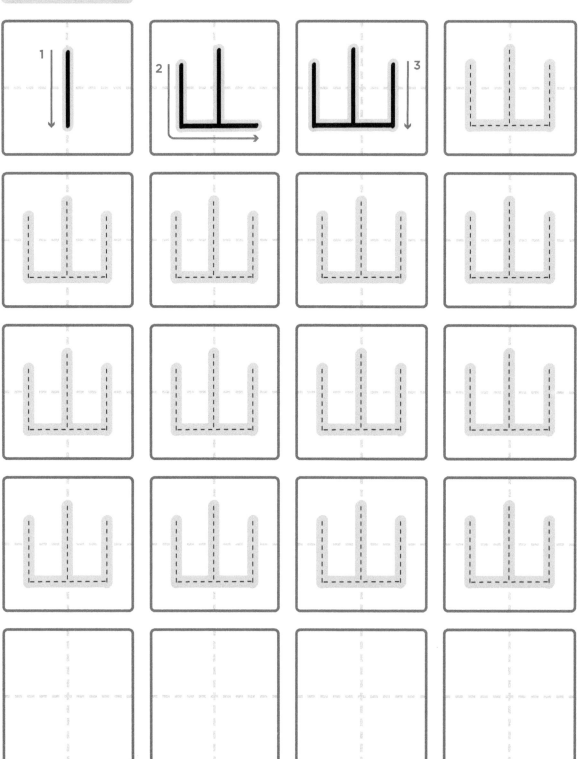

Character: 川
English: river
Strokes: 3
Pinyin: *chuān*

TIP
The three strokes in this character look like a flowing river.

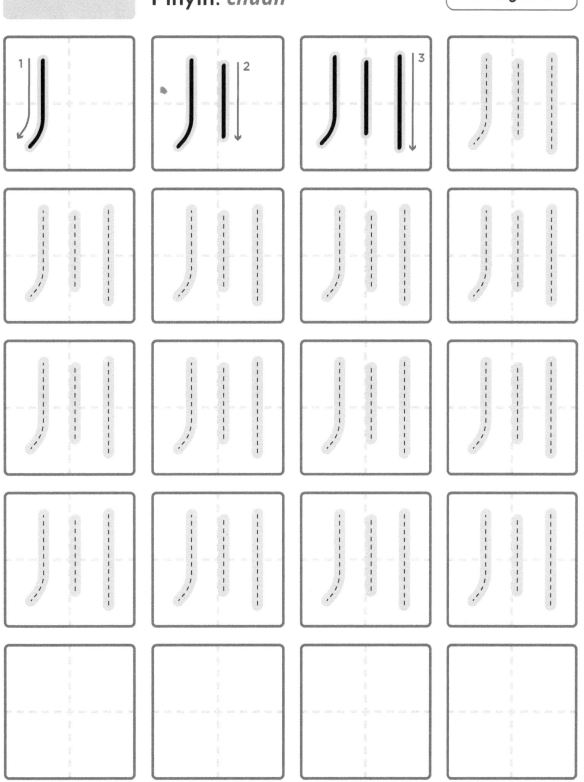

Character: 土
English: ground/soil
Strokes: 3
Pinyin: *tǔ*

TIP

The bottom stroke is the ground. There's a flower growing from it!

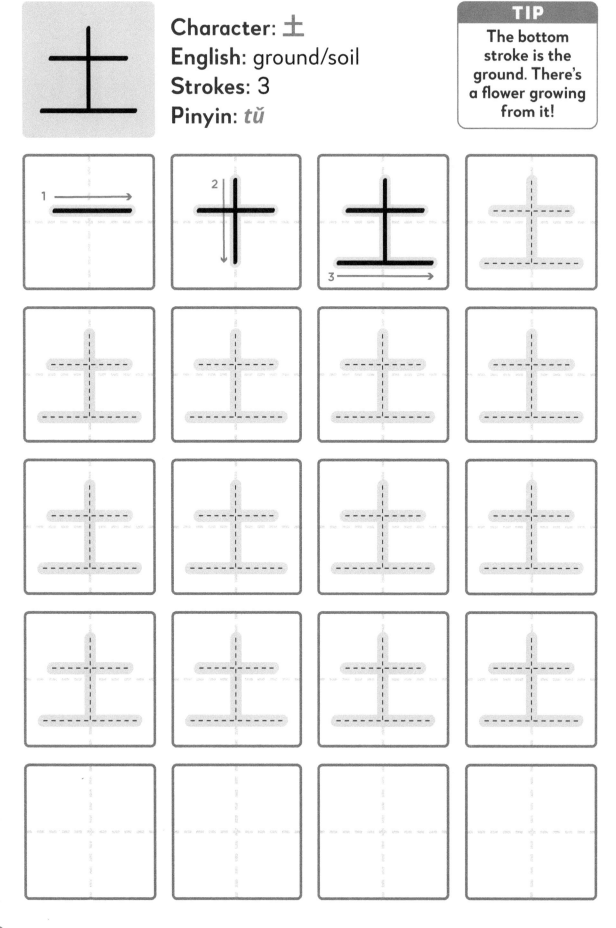

Character: 门
English: door
Strokes: 3
Pinyin: *mén*

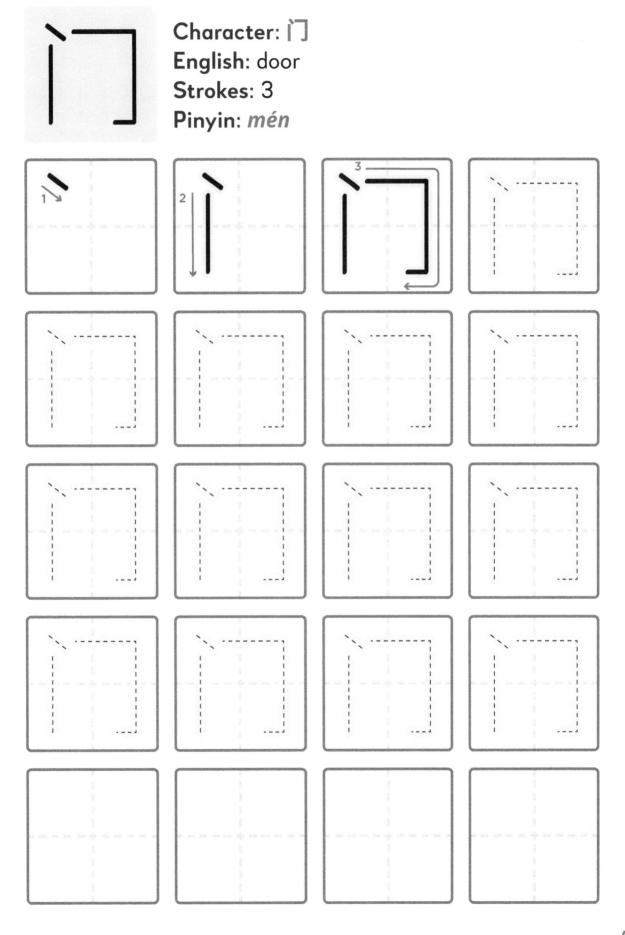

Character: 工
English: work
Strokes: 3
Pinyin: *gōng*

Character: 口
English: mouth
Strokes: 3
Pinyin: *kǒu*

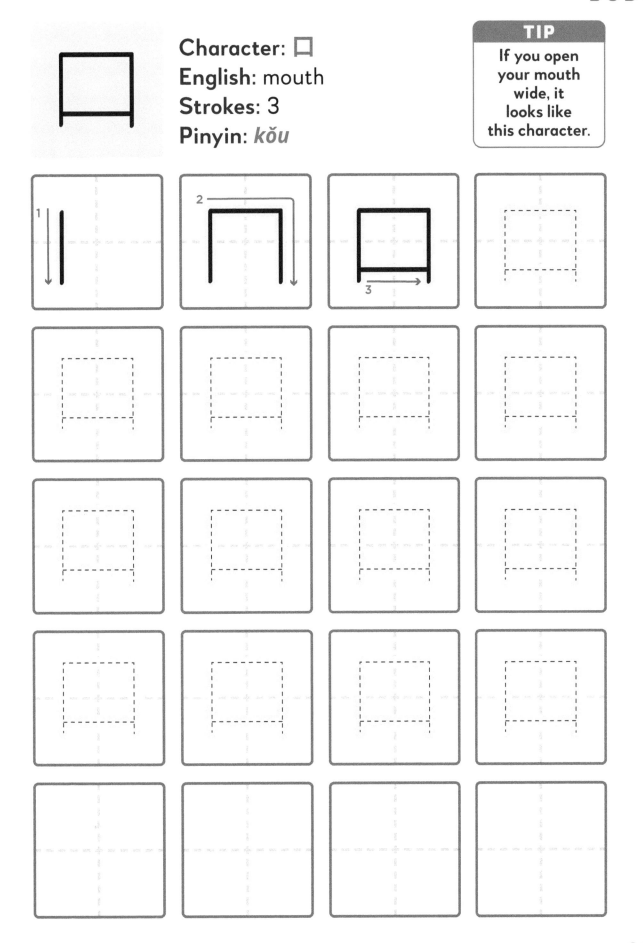

Character: 马
English: horse
Strokes: 3
Pinyin: *mǎ*

CHINESE CHARACTER PRACTICE WORKBOOK FOR KIDS

Character: 子
English: child
Strokes: 3
Pinyin: *zǐ*

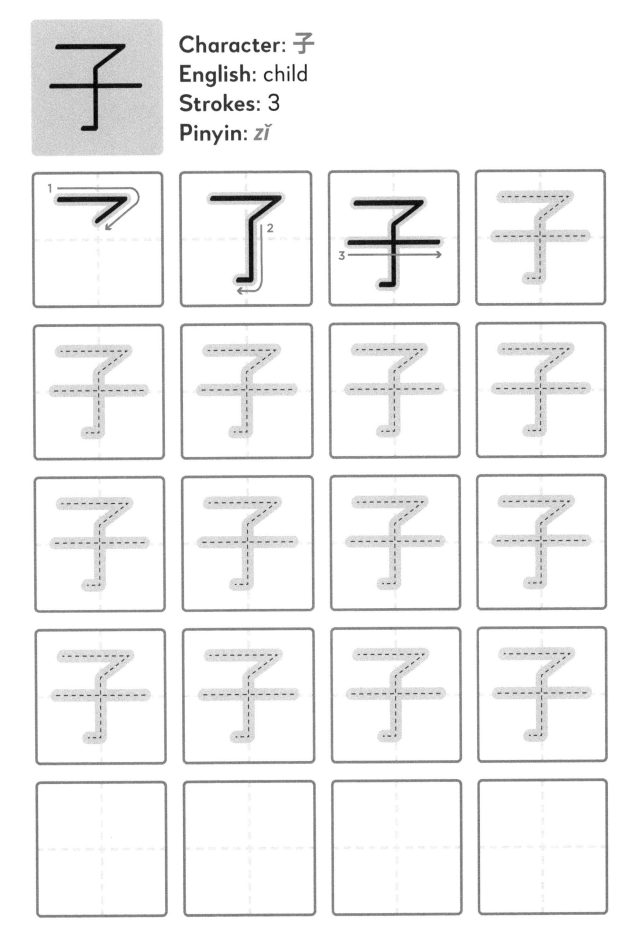

Character: 女
English: female/woman
Strokes: 3
Pinyin: *nǔ*

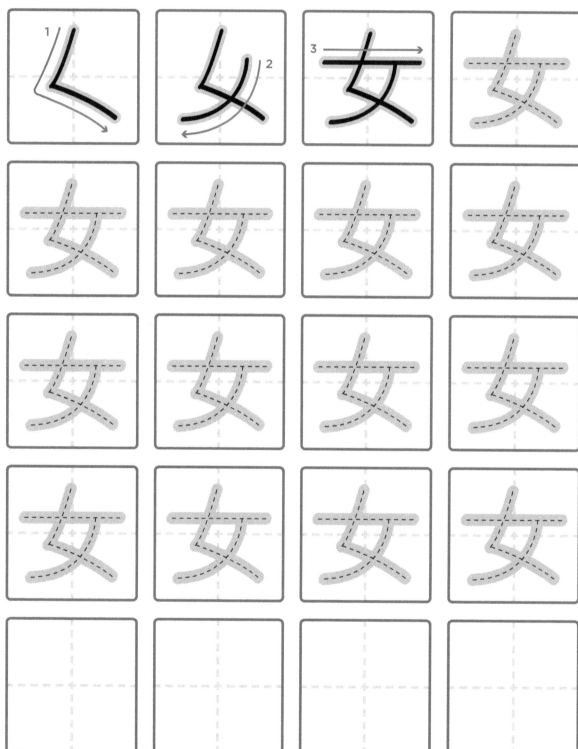

Character: 飞
English: fly
Strokes: 3
Pinyin: *fēi*

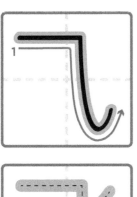   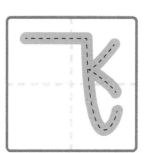

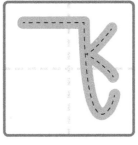   

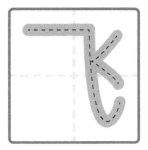 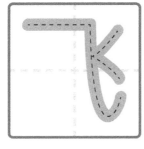 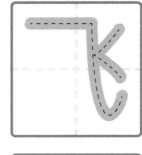 

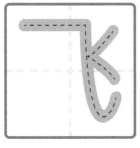 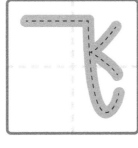 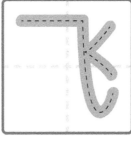 

Character: 个
English: measure word
Strokes: 3
Pinyin: *gè*

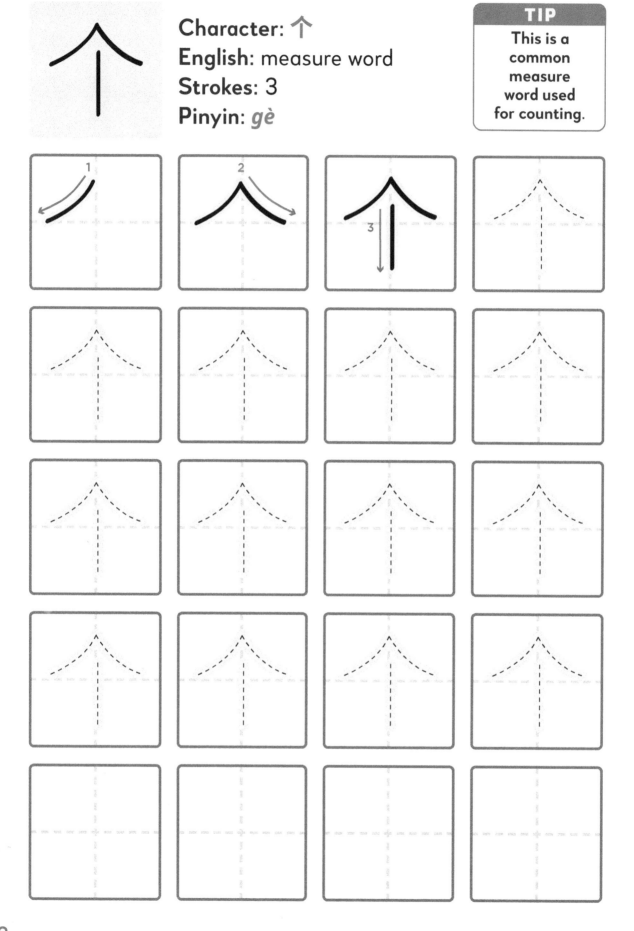

CHINESE CHARACTER PRACTICE WORKBOOK FOR KIDS

Character: 上
English: up
Strokes: 3
Pinyin: *shàng*

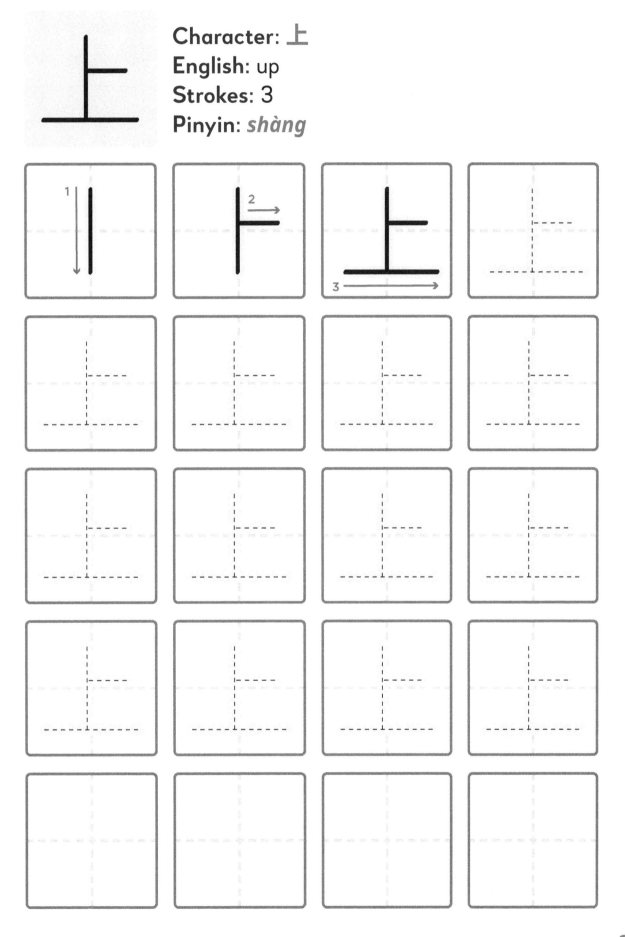

Character: 下
English: down
Strokes: 3
Pinyin: *xià*

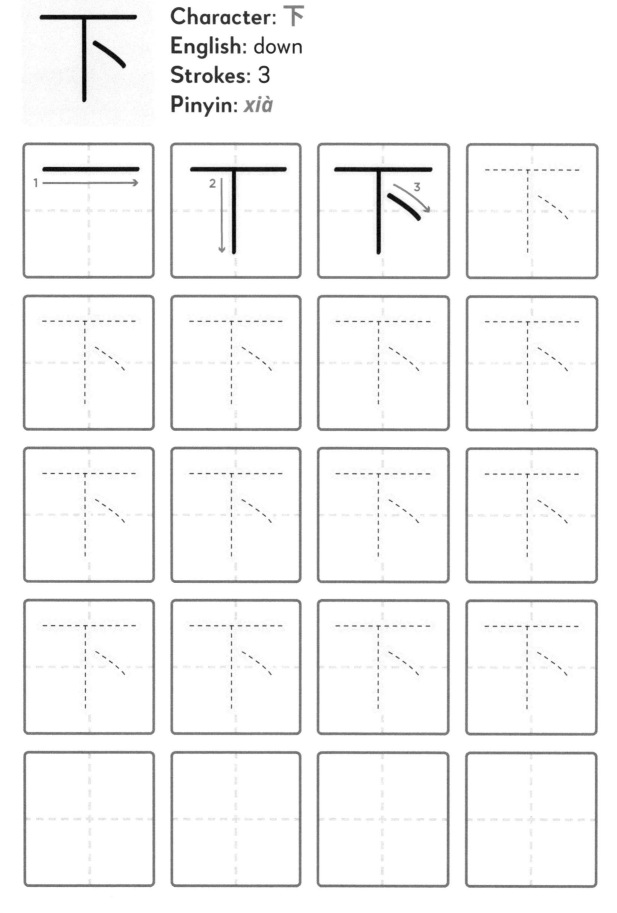

CHINESE CHARACTER PRACTICE WORKBOOK FOR KIDS

Character: 月
English: moon/month
Strokes: 4
Pinyin: *yuè*

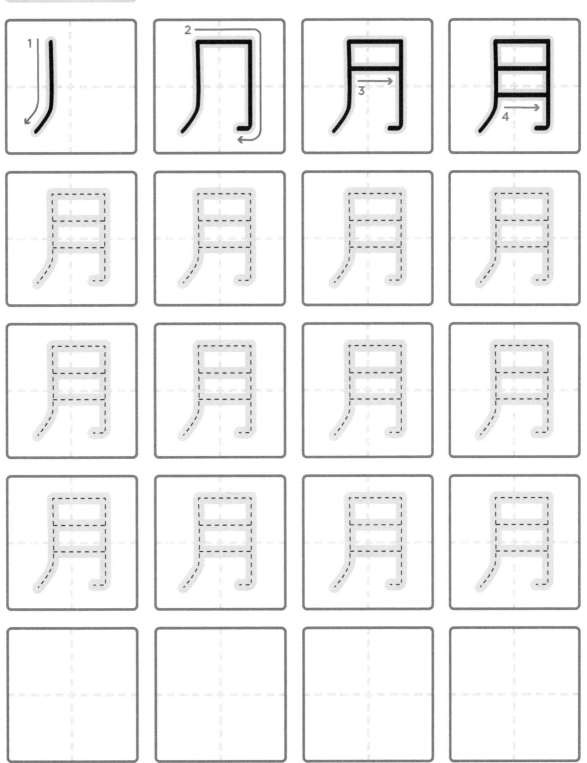

Character: 日
English: sun/day
Strokes: 4
Pinyin: *rì*

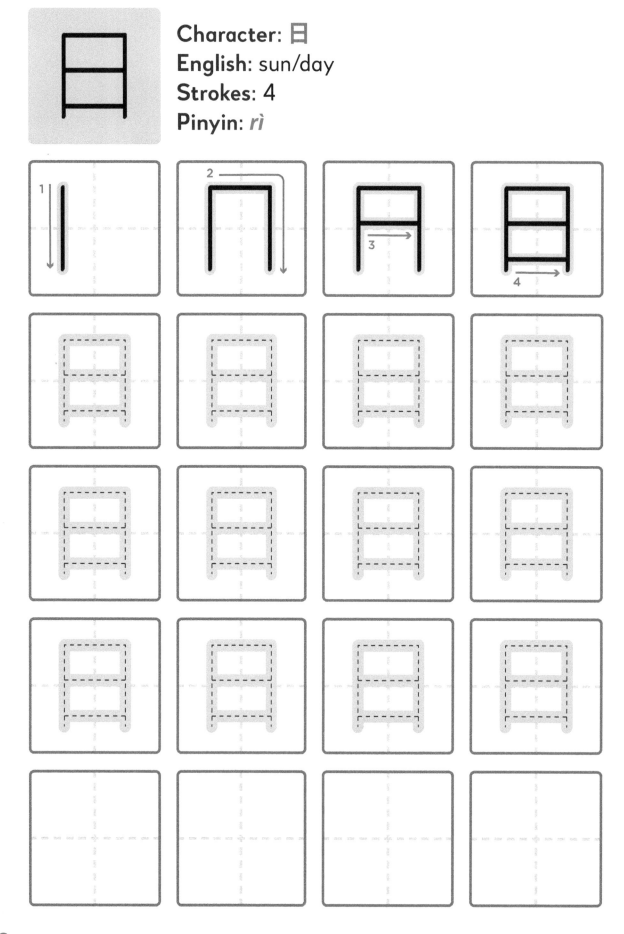

CHINESE CHARACTER PRACTICE WORKBOOK FOR KIDS

Character: 木
English: tree/wood
Strokes: 4
Pinyin: *mù*

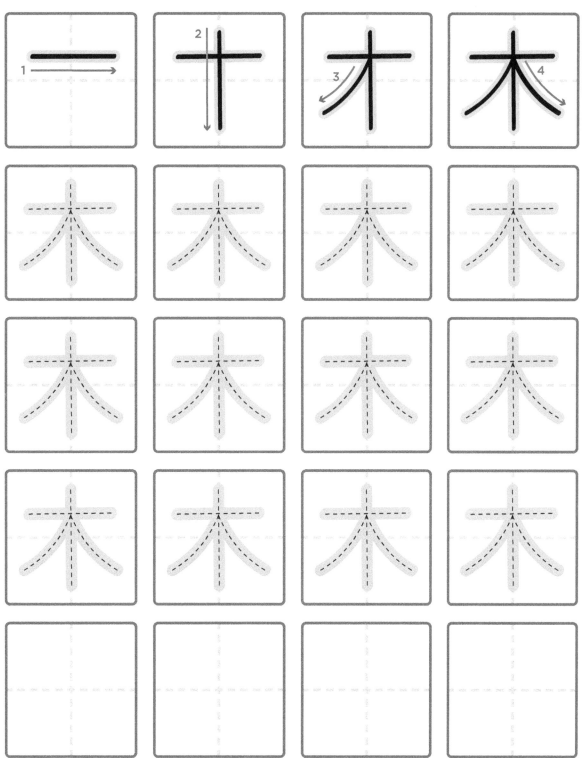

Character: 水
English: water
Strokes: 4
Pinyin: *shuǐ*

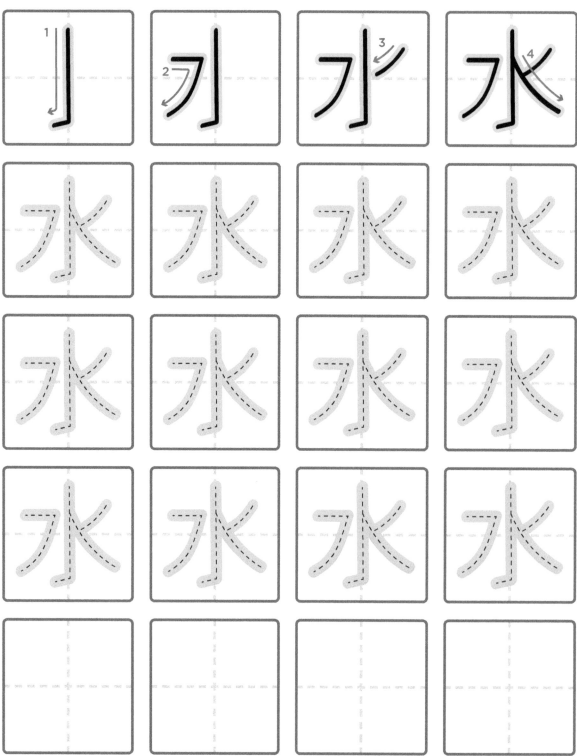

CHINESE CHARACTER PRACTICE WORKBOOK FOR KIDS

Character: 天
English: sky
Strokes: 4
Pinyin: *tiān*

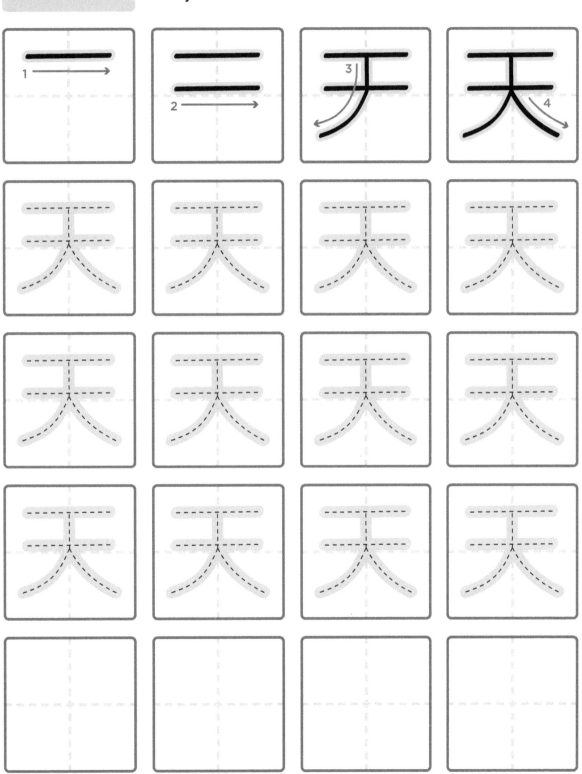

Character: 火
English: fire
Strokes: 4
Pinyin: *huǒ*

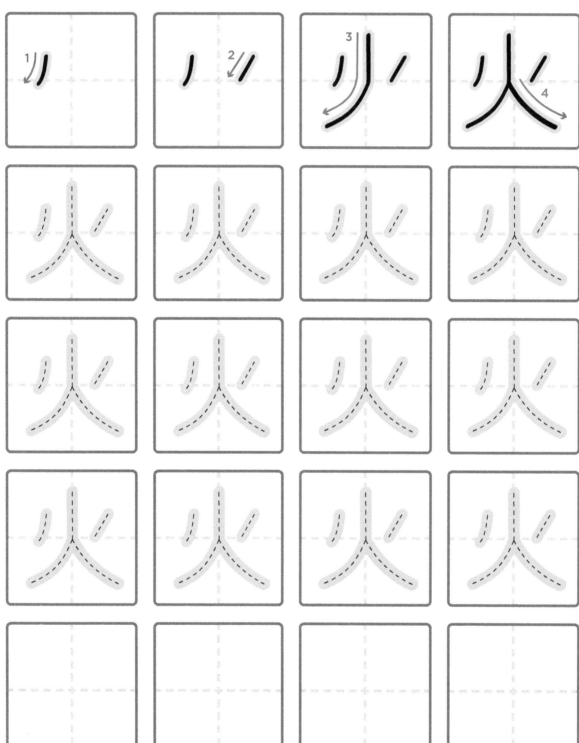

CHINESE CHARACTER PRACTICE WORKBOOK FOR KIDS

Character: 风
English: wind
Strokes: 4
Pinyin: *fēng*

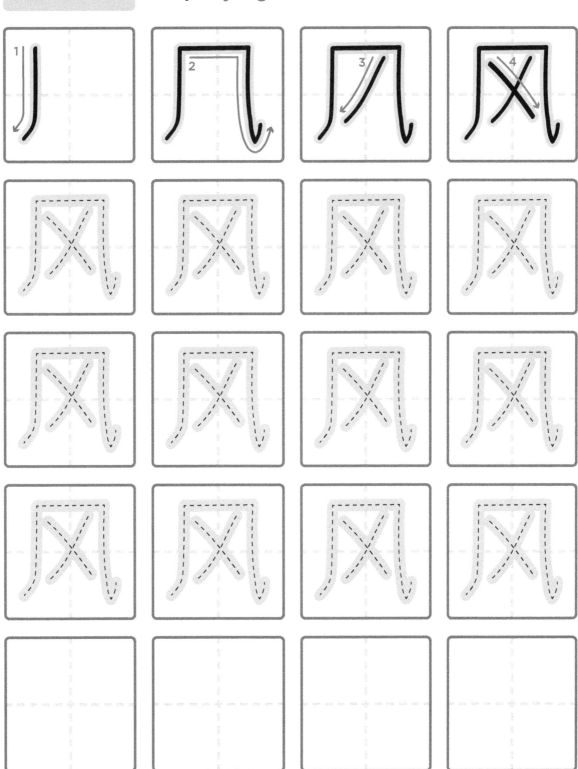

Character: 气
English: air
Strokes: 4
Pinyin: *qì*

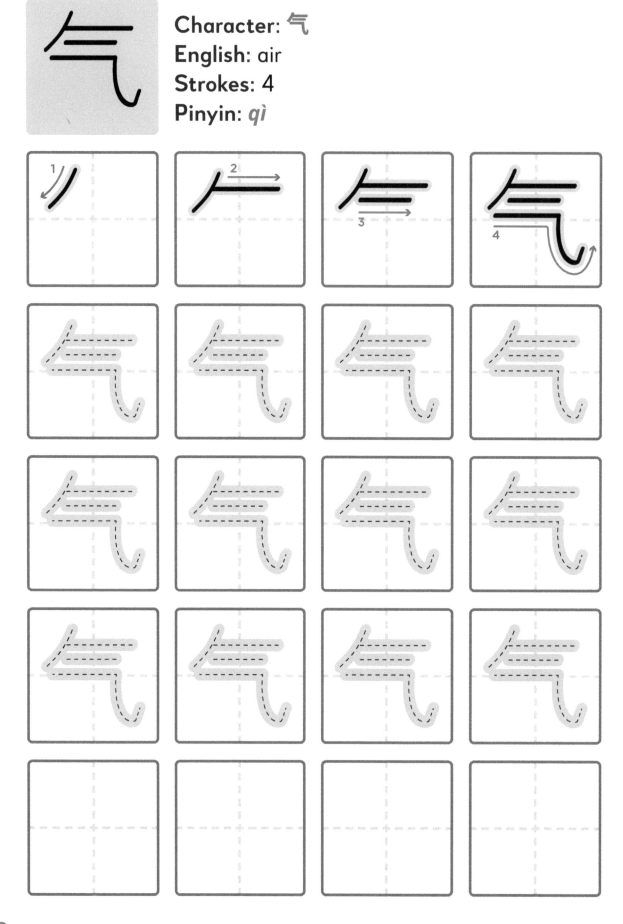

Character: 云
English: cloud
Strokes: 4
Pinyin: *yún*

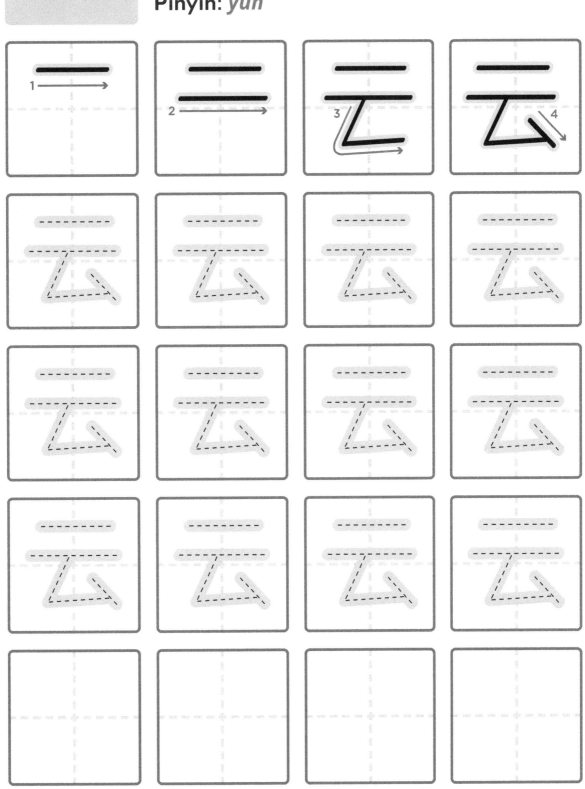

Character: 牛
English: cow
Strokes: 4
Pinyin: *niú*

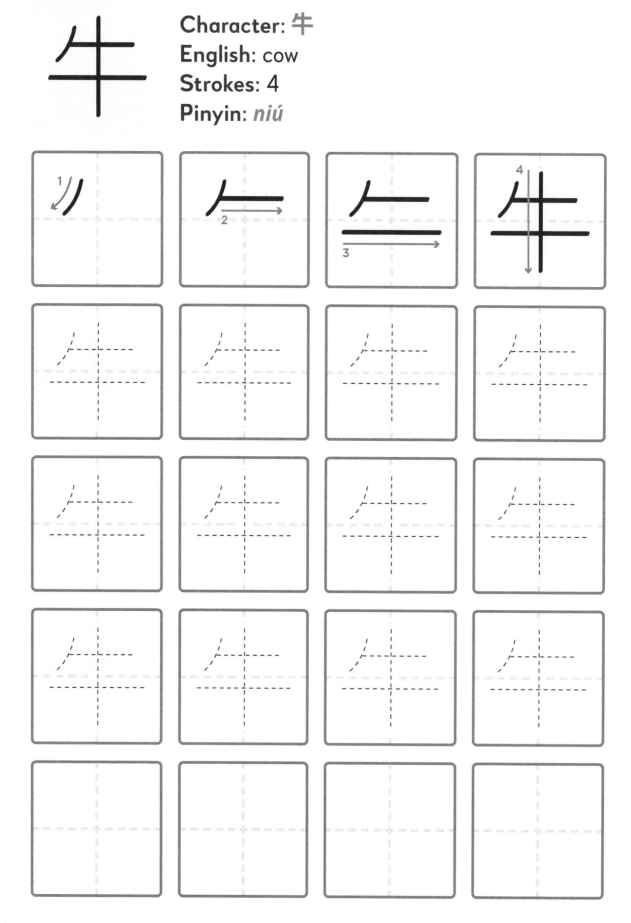

Character: 心
English: heart
Strokes: 4
Pinyin: *xīn*

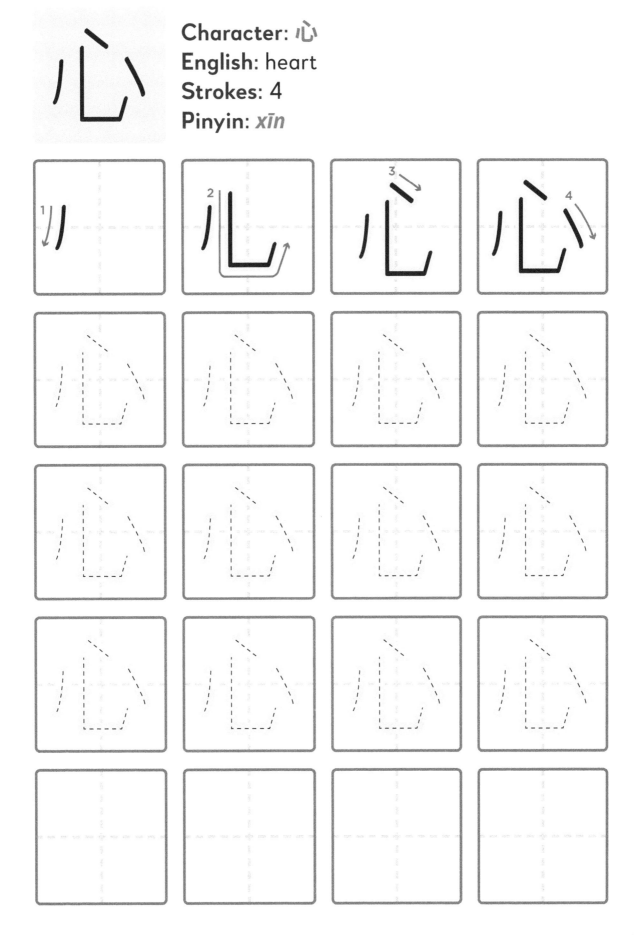

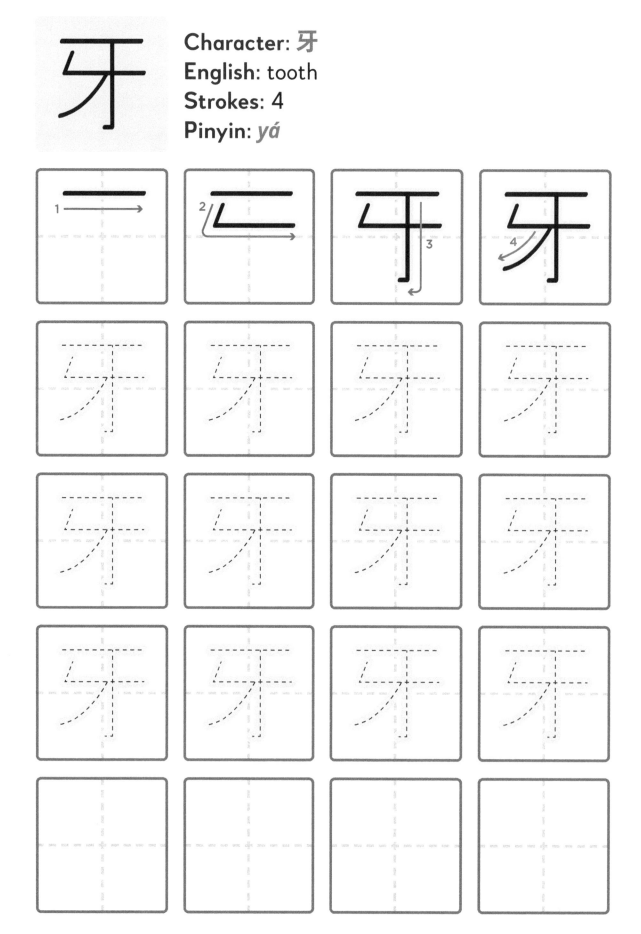

Character: 牙
English: tooth
Strokes: 4
Pinyin: *yá*

Character: 手
English: hand
Strokes: 4
Pinyin: *shǒu*

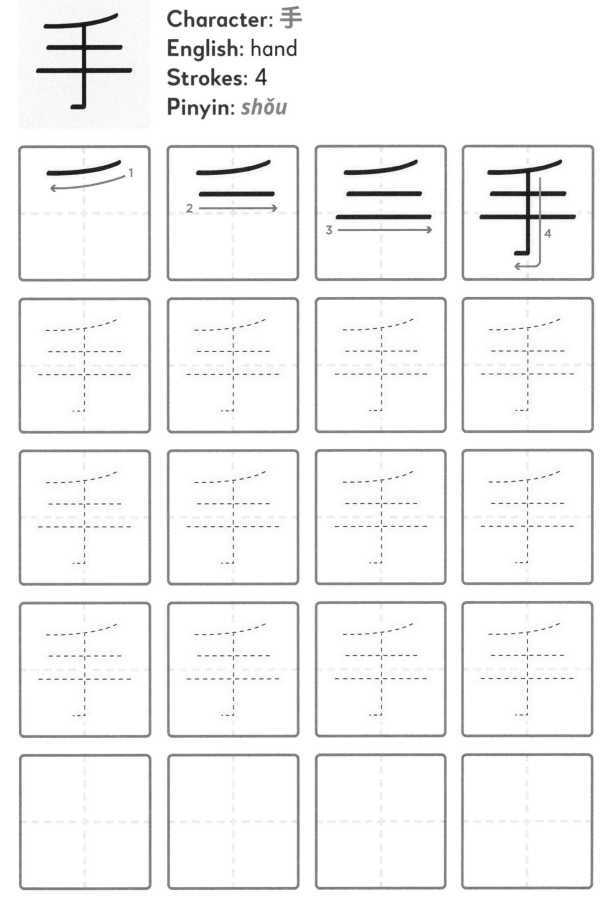

Character: 父
English: father
Strokes: 4
Pinyin: *fù*

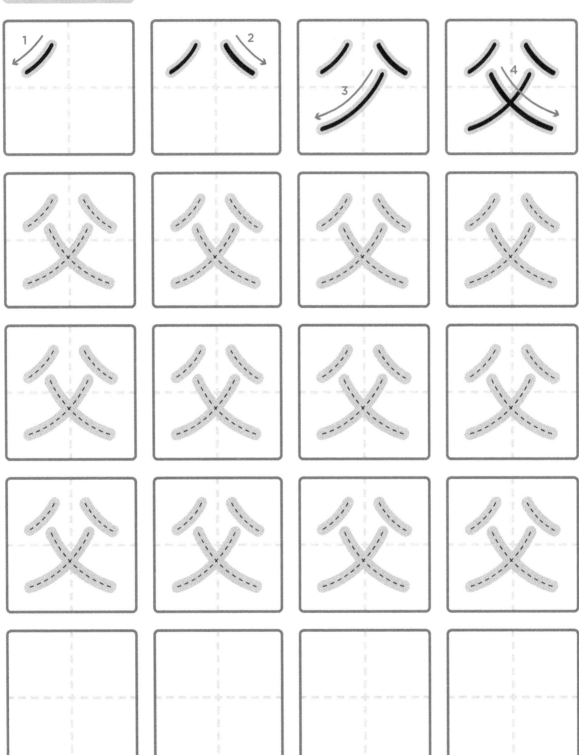

Character: 王
English: king
Strokes: 4
Pinyin: *wáng*

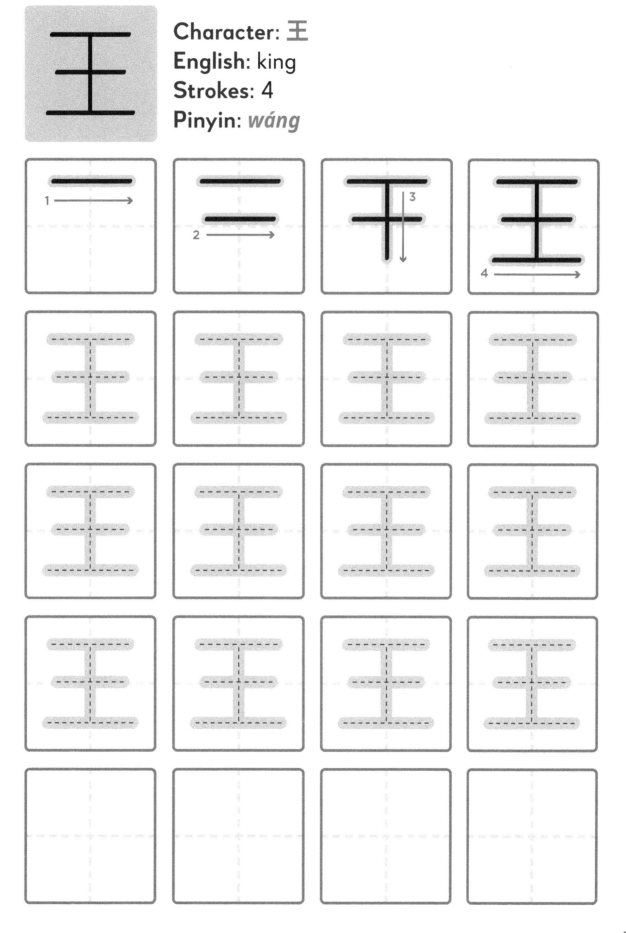

Character: 友
English: friend
Strokes: 4
Pinyin: *yǒu*

CHINESE CHARACTER PRACTICE WORKBOOK FOR KIDS

Character: 书
English: book
Strokes: 4
Pinyin: *shū*

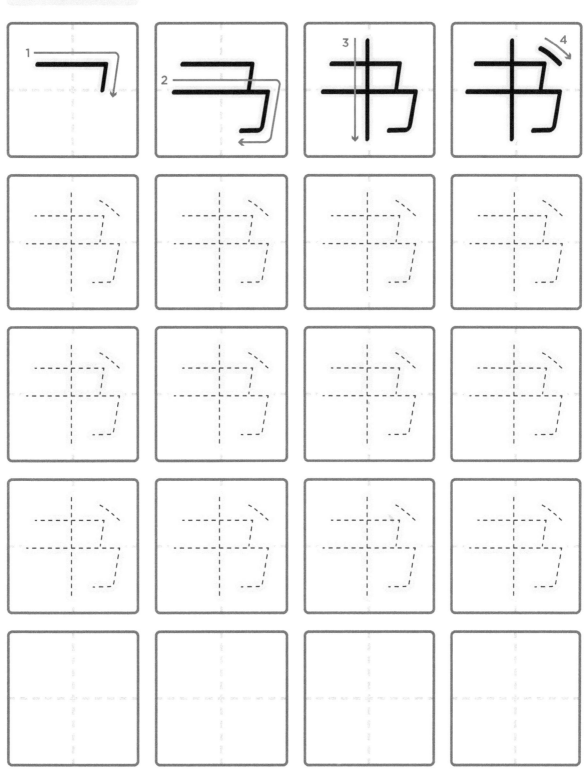

Character: 开
English: open
Strokes: 4
Pinyin: *kāi*

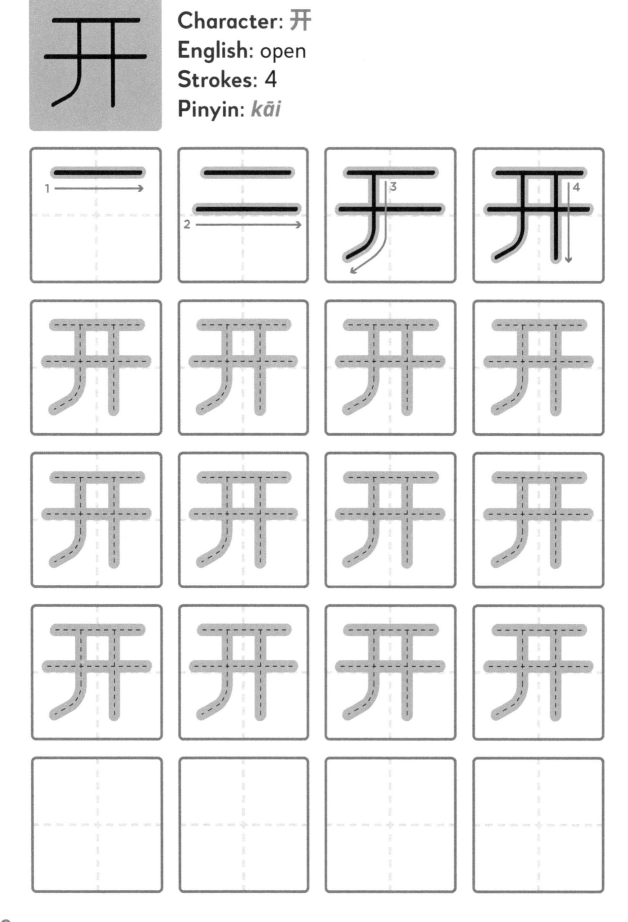

CHINESE CHARACTER PRACTICE WORKBOOK FOR KIDS

Character: 长
English: grow
Strokes: 4
Pinyin: *zhǎng*

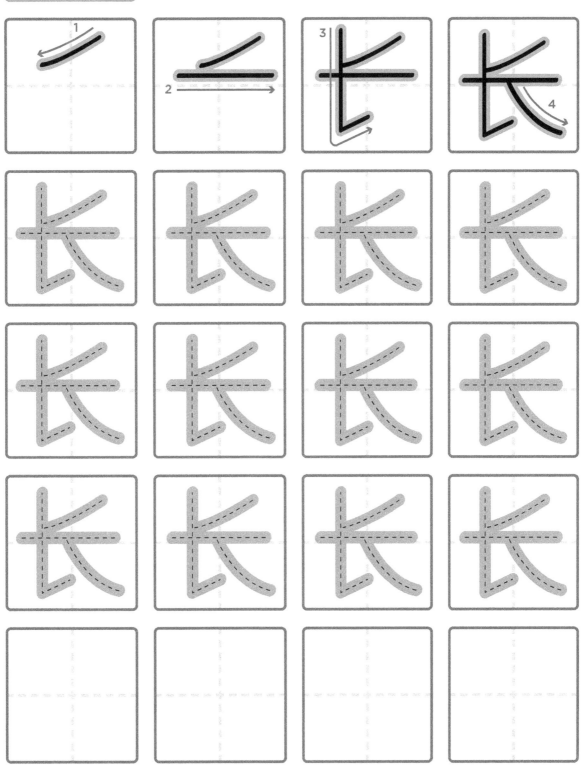

Character: 中
English: middle
Strokes: 4
Pinyin: *zhōng*

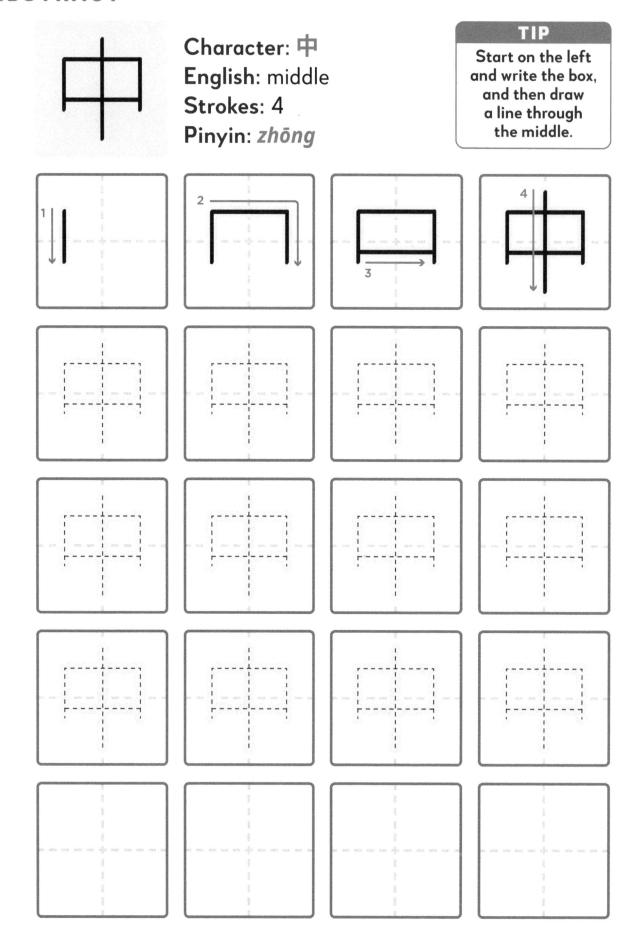

Character: 车
English: car
Strokes: 4
Pinyin: *chē*

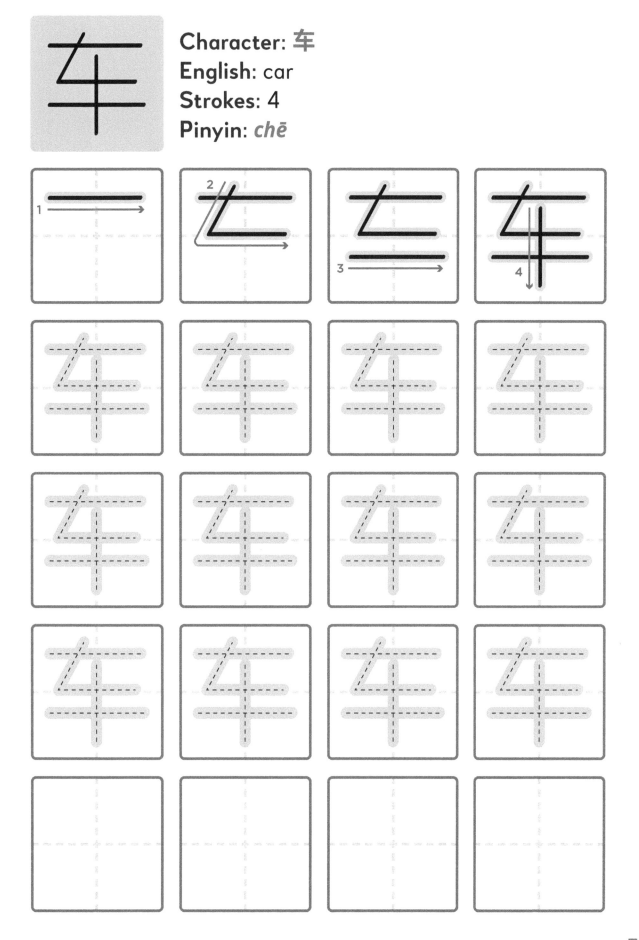

Character: 不
English: no/not
Strokes: 4
Pinyin: *bù*

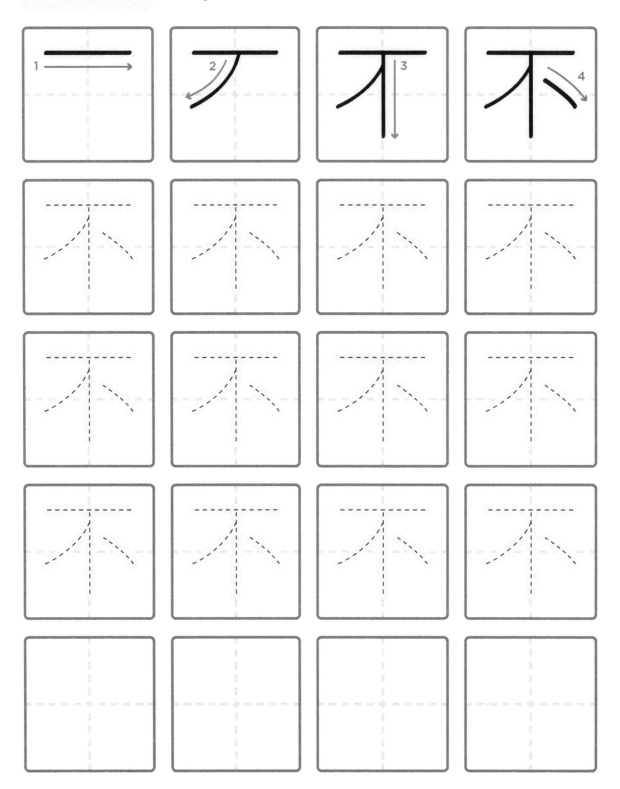

Character: 白
English: white
Strokes: 5
Pinyin: *bái*

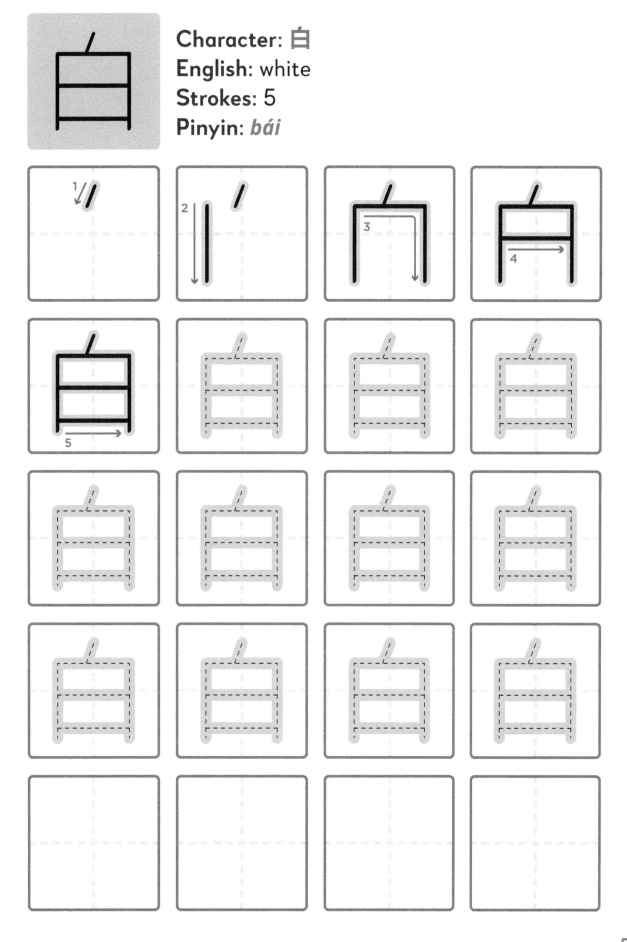

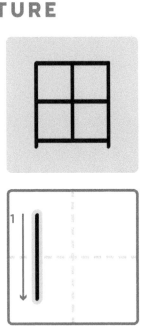

Character: 田
English: field
Strokes: 5
Pinyin: *tián*

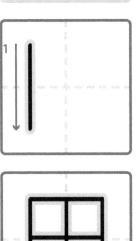
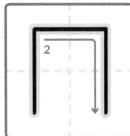
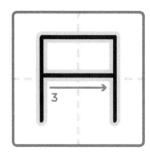
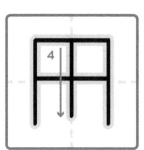

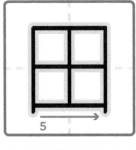
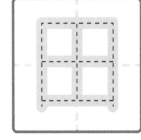
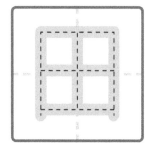
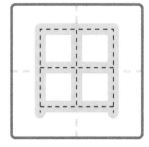

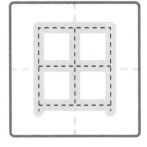
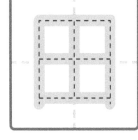
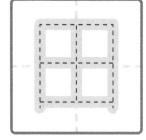
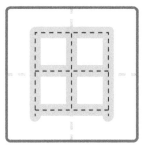

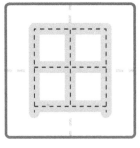
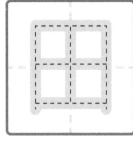
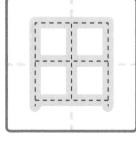
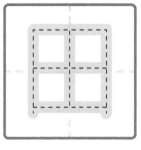

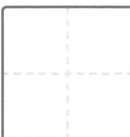

Character: 禾
English: grain
Strokes: 5
Pinyin: *hé*

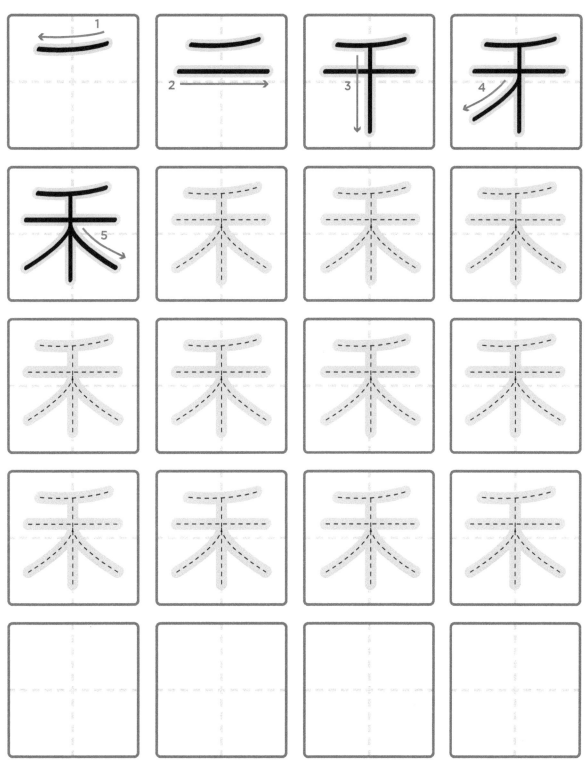

Character: 叶
English: leaf
Strokes: 5
Pinyin: *yè*

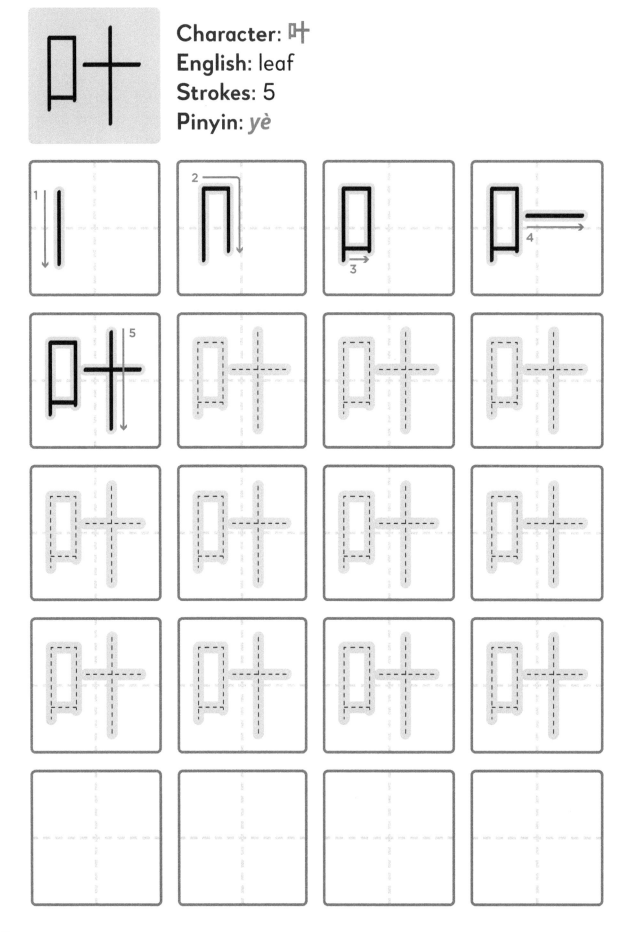

CHINESE CHARACTER PRACTICE WORKBOOK FOR KIDS

Character: 冬
English: winter
Strokes: 5
Pinyin: *dōng*

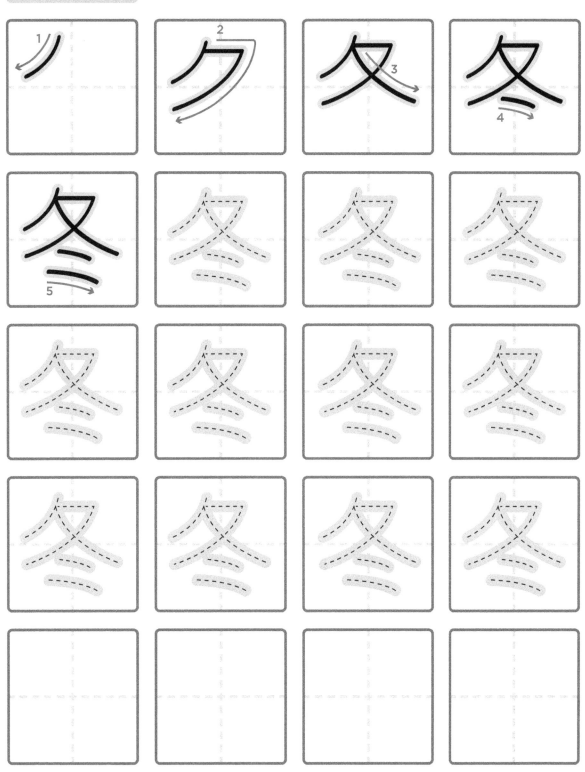

Character: 鸟
English: bird
Strokes: 5
Pinyin: *niǎo*

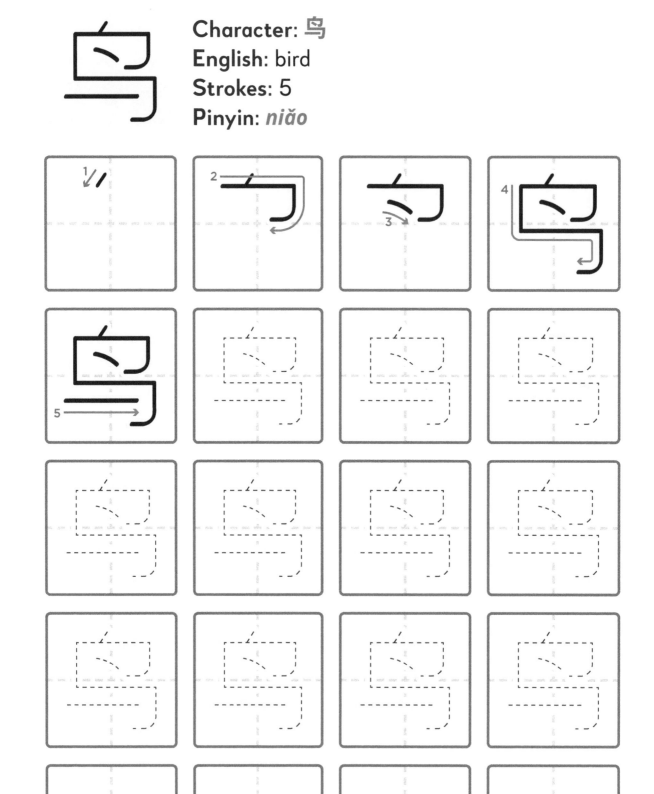

CHINESE CHARACTER PRACTICE WORKBOOK FOR KIDS

Character: 龙
English: dragon
Strokes: 5
Pinyin: *lóng*

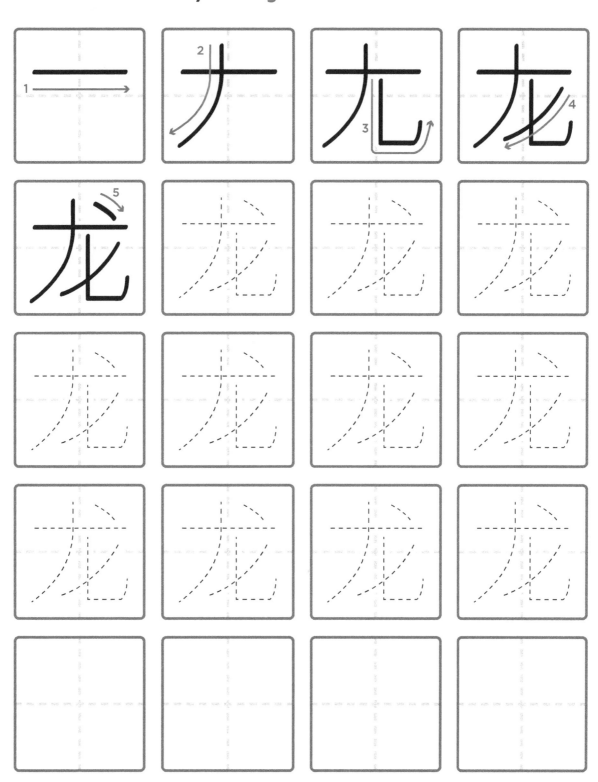

Character: 左
English: left
Strokes: 5
Pinyin: *zuǒ*

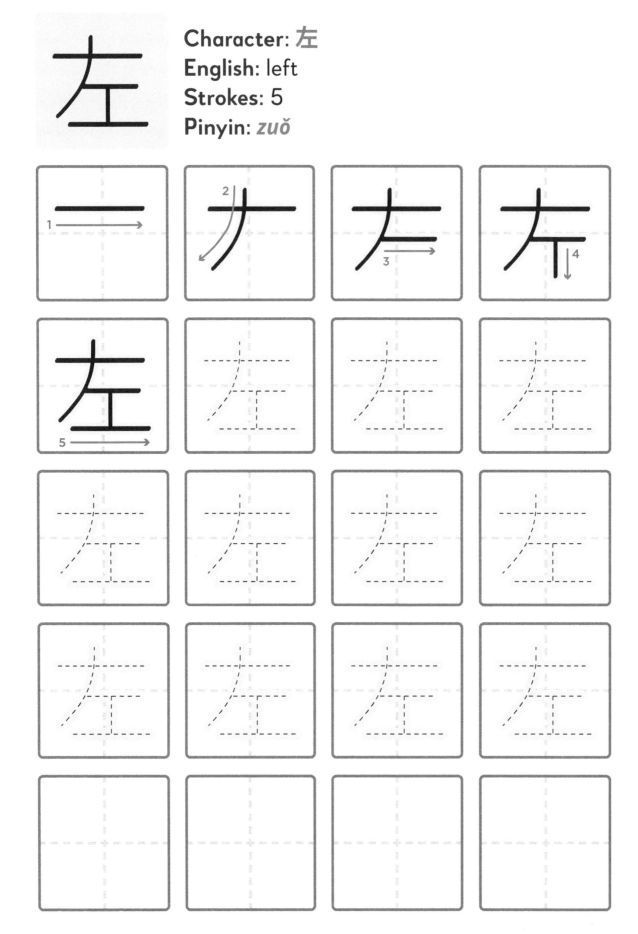

Character: 右
English: right
Strokes: 5
Pinyin: *yòu*

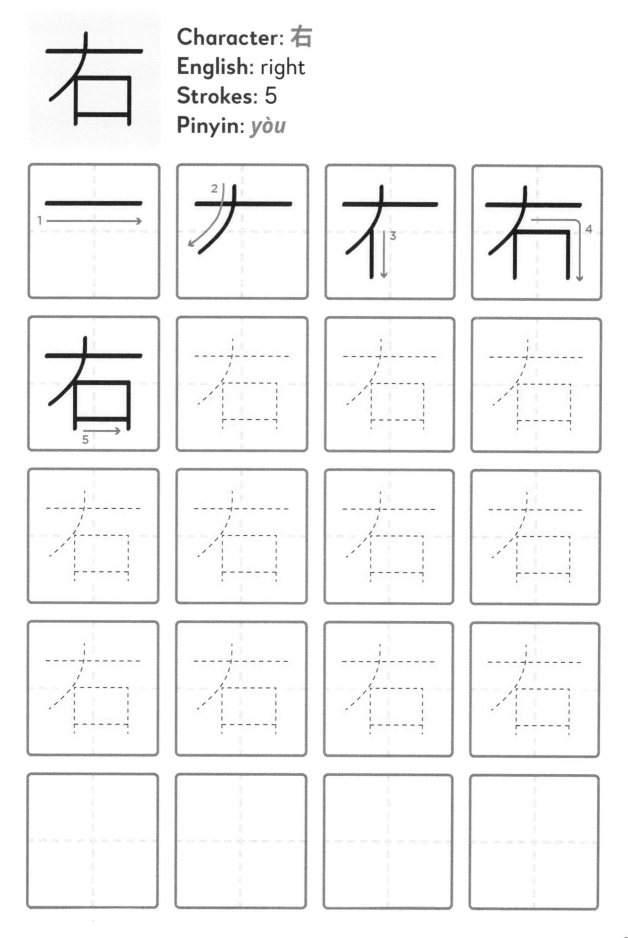

Character: 头
English: head
Strokes: 5
Pinyin: *tóu*

TIP
Draw the two strokes on the side first (丶), then it's just the character for big (大)!

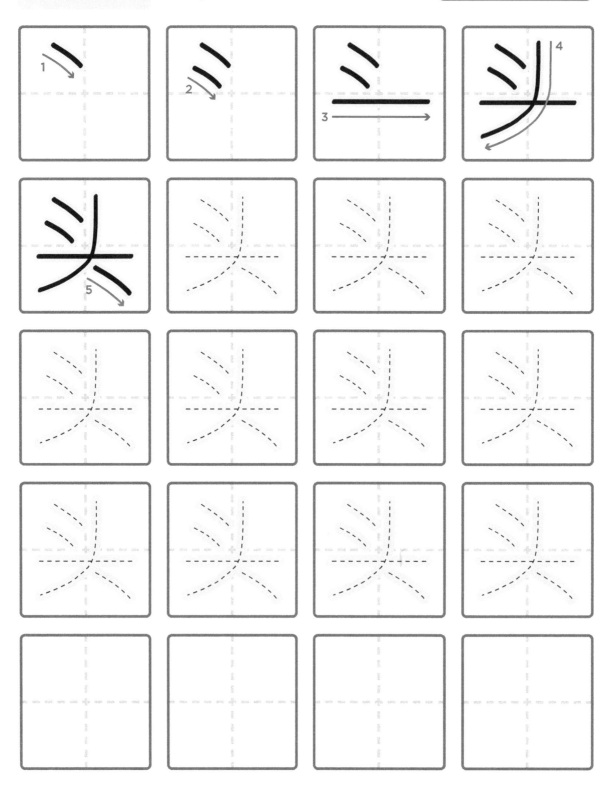

Character: 目
English: eye
Strokes: 5
Pinyin: *mù*

TIP

Don't forget to start the outside of the box on the left with one line top to bottom.

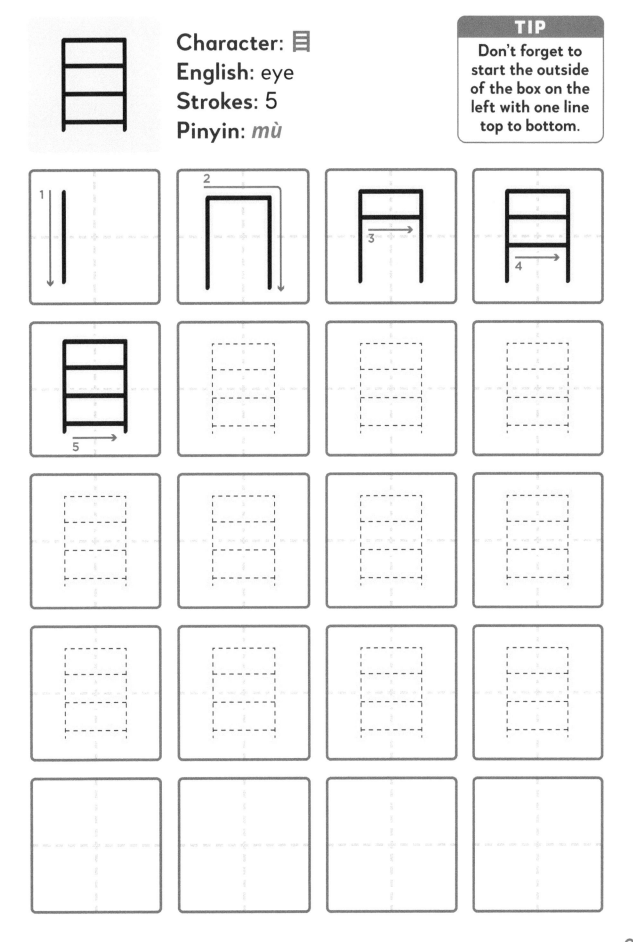

Character: 生
English: birth
Strokes: 5
Pinyin: *shēng*

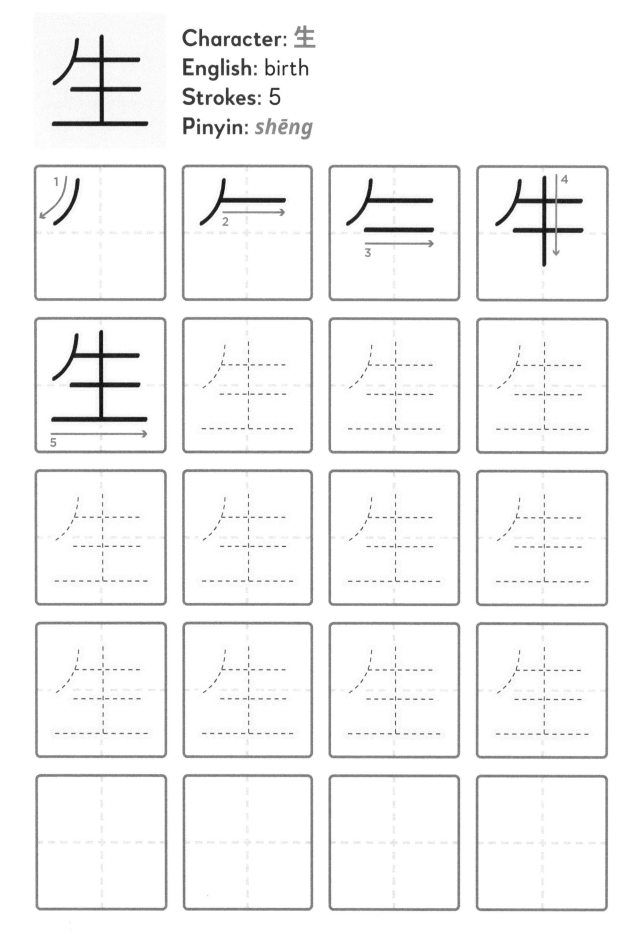

Character: 包
English: bag/package
Strokes: 5
Pinyin: *bāo*

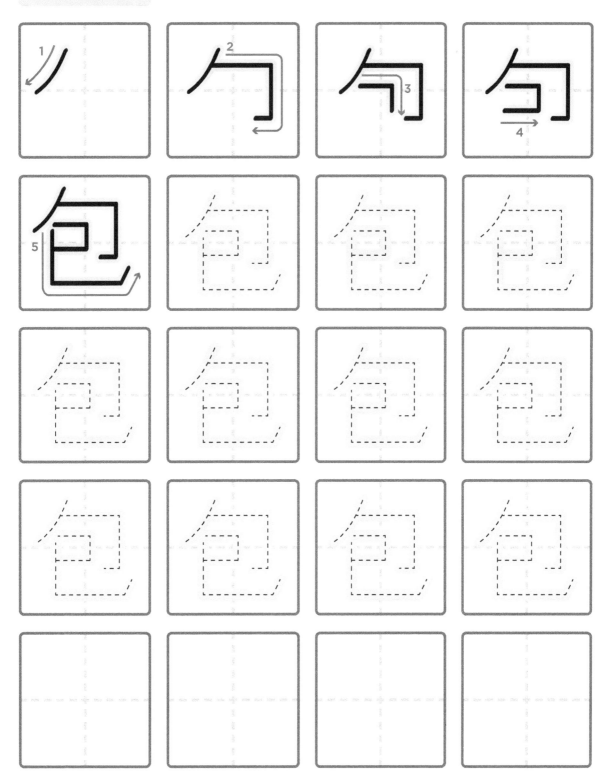

Character: 写
English: write
Strokes: 5
Pinyin: *xiě*

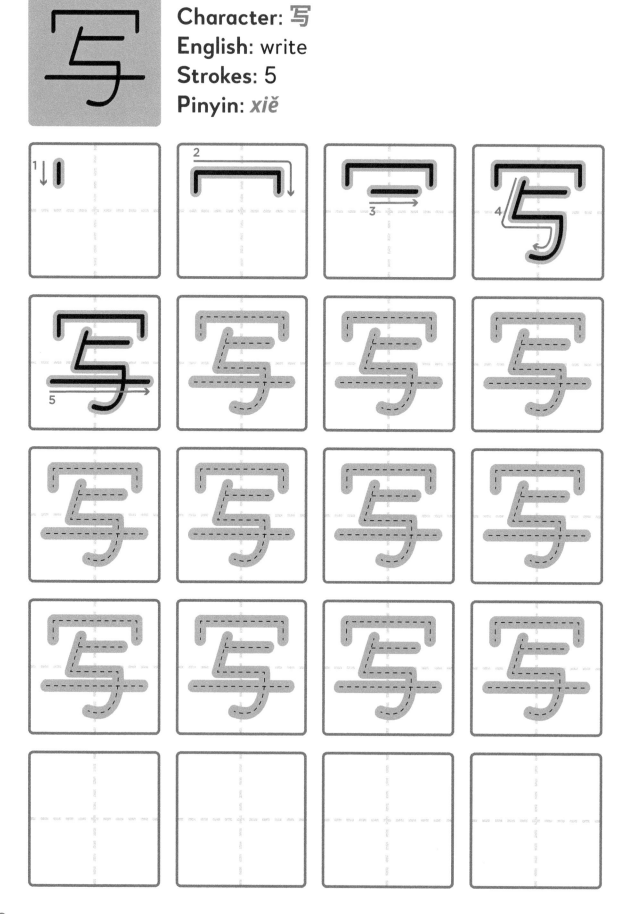

Character: 去
English: go
Strokes: 5
Pinyin: *qù*

Character: 囚
English: prisoner
Strokes: 5
Pinyin: *qiú*

TIP

First, write the enclosure (囗). Then, write the person (人) inside.

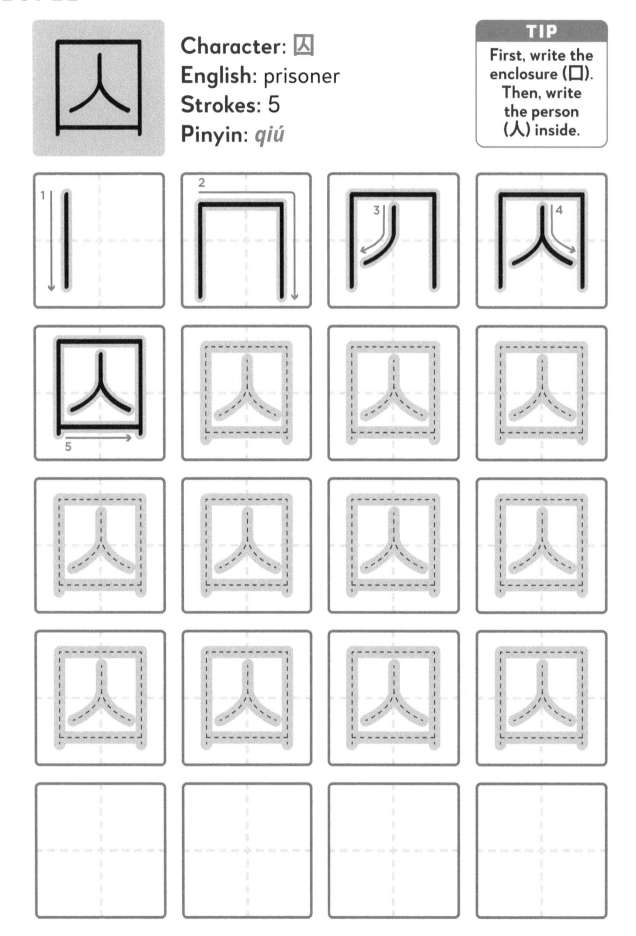

Character: 他
English: he/him
Strokes: 5
Pinyin: *tā*

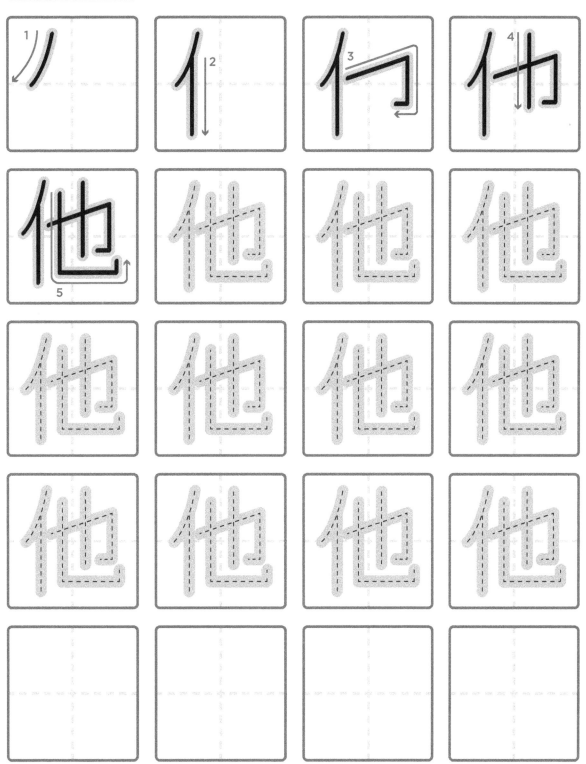

Character: 乐
English: happy
Strokes: 5
Pinyin: *lè*

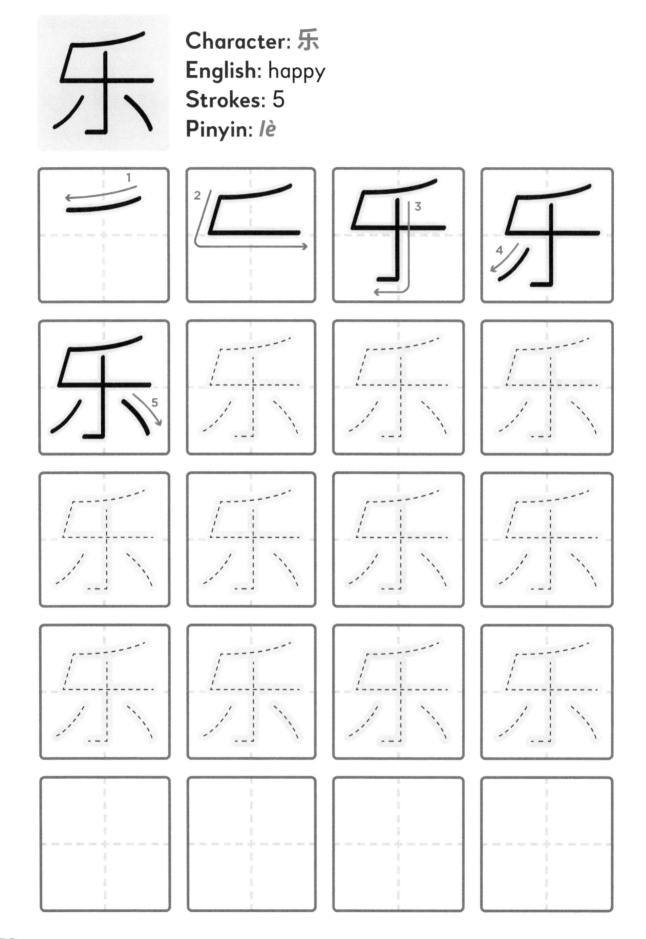

CHINESE CHARACTER PRACTICE WORKBOOK FOR KIDS

Character: 用
English: use
Strokes: 5
Pinyin: *yòng*

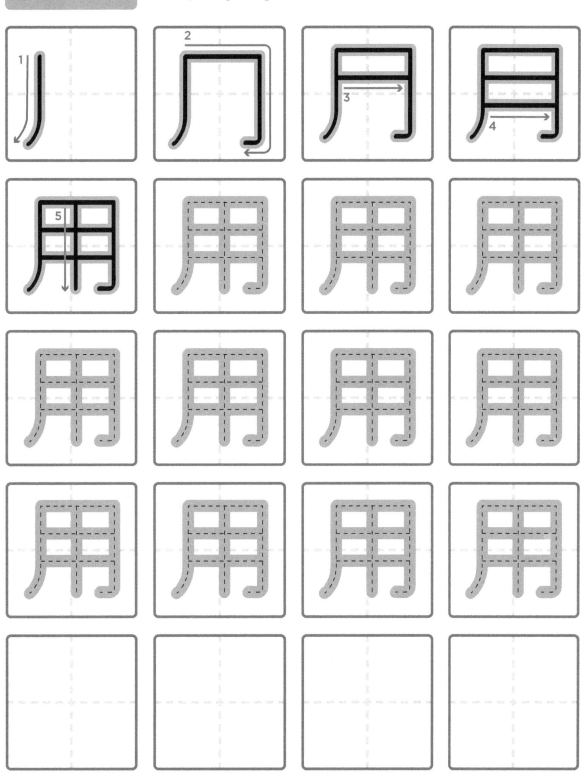

Character: 对
English: correct
Strokes: 5
Pinyin: *duì*

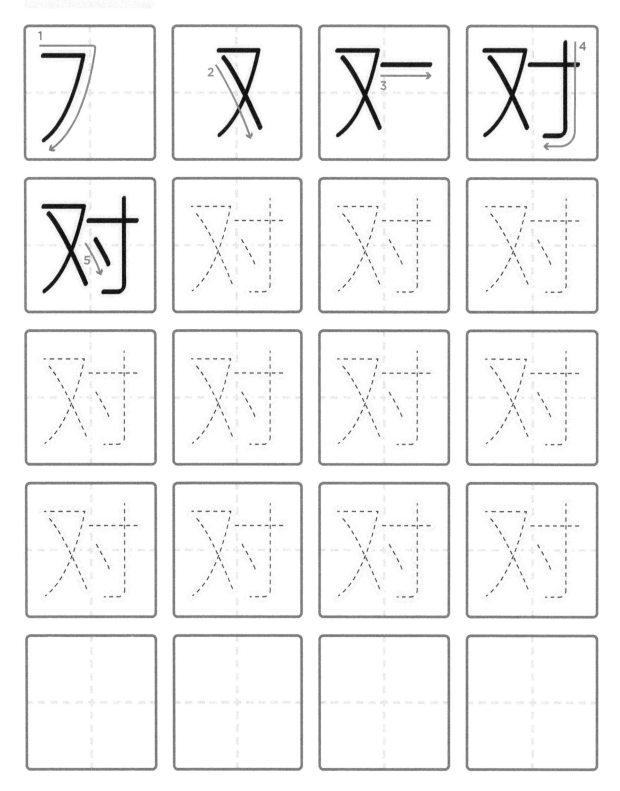

Character: 百
English: hundred
Strokes: 6
Pinyin: *bǎi*

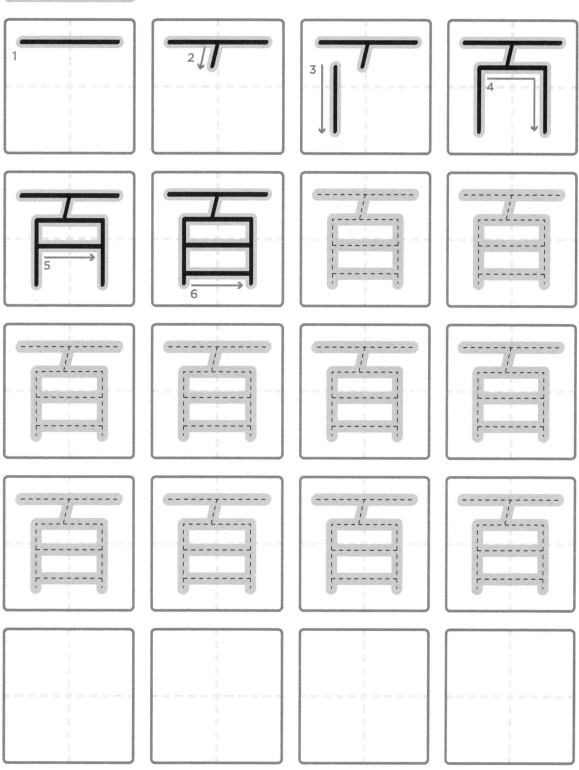

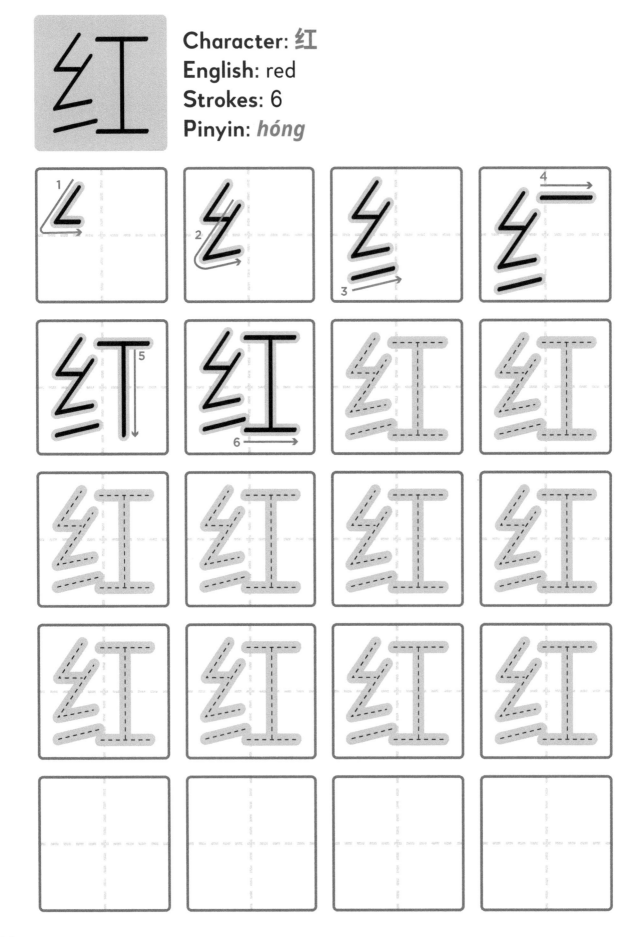

Character: 红
English: red
Strokes: 6
Pinyin: *hóng*

Character: 色
English: color
Strokes: 6
Pinyin: *sè*

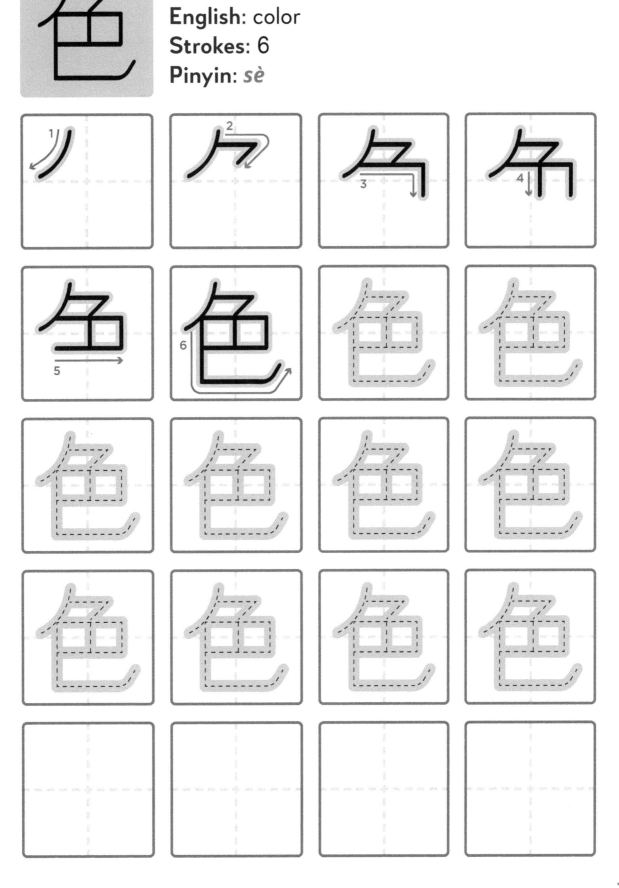

Character: 米
English: rice
Strokes: 6
Pinyin: *mǐ*

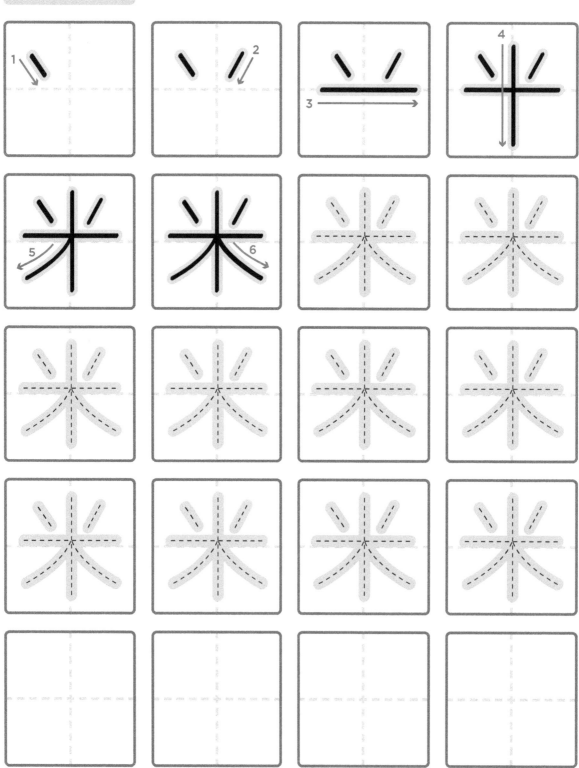

Character: 地
English: earth/ground
Strokes: 6
Pinyin: *dì*

 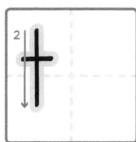  

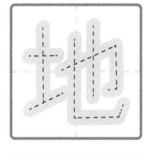 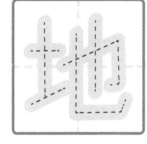 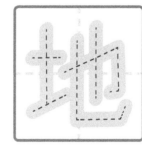 

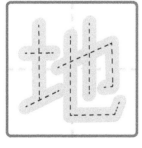 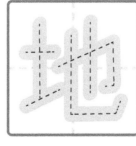 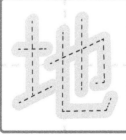 

Character: 竹
English: bamboo
Strokes: 6
Pinyin: *zhú*

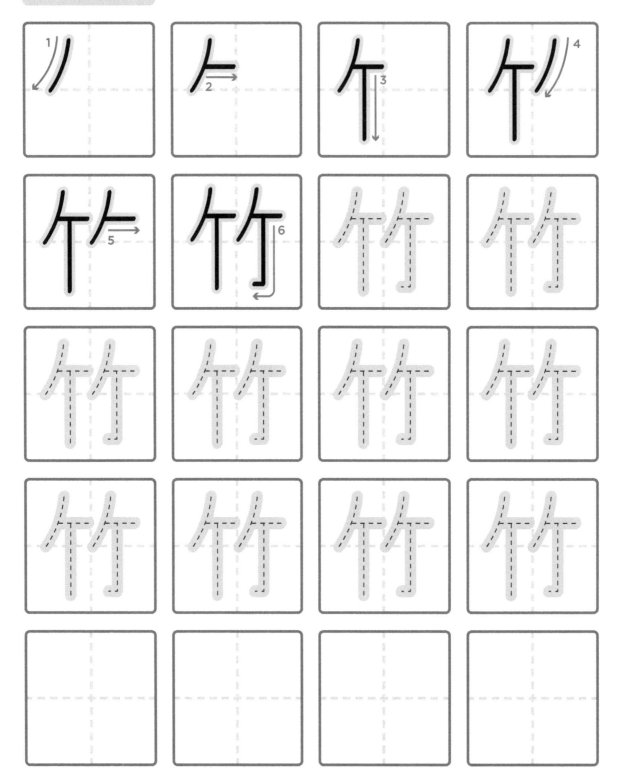

Character: 早
English: morning
Strokes: 6
Pinyin: *zǎo*

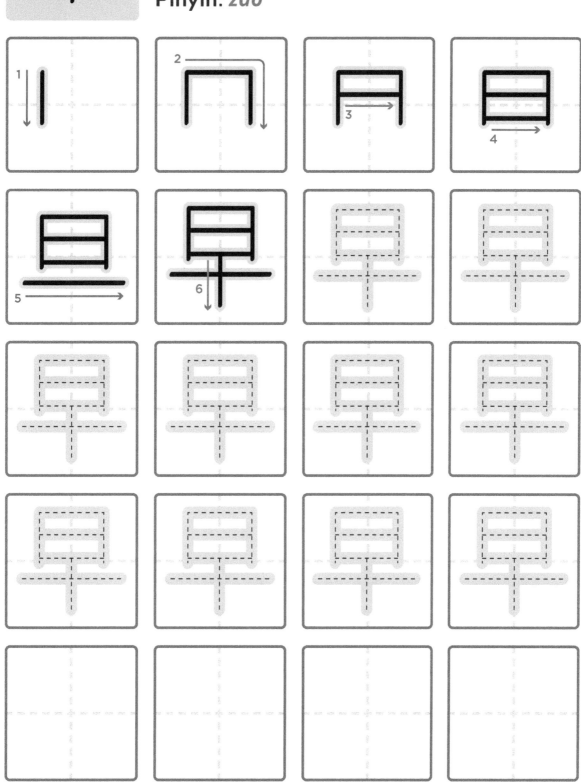

Character: 羊
English: sheep
Strokes: 6
Pinyin: *yáng*

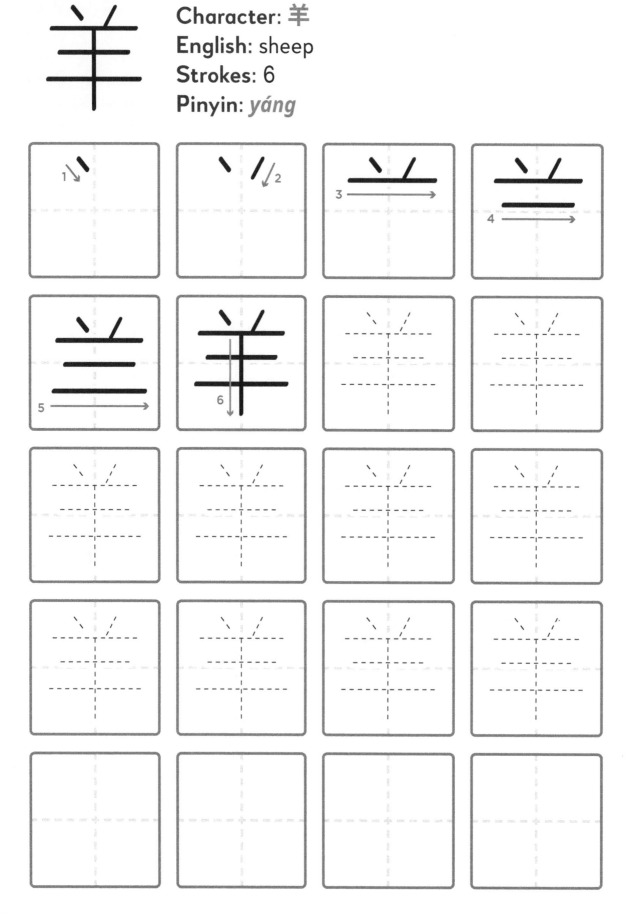

Character: 耳
English: ear
Strokes: 6
Pinyin: *ěr*

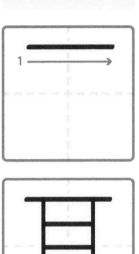
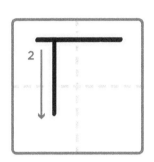
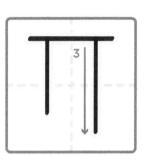

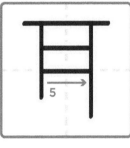

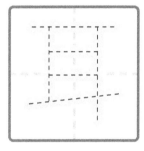
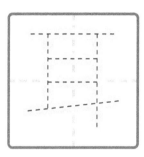
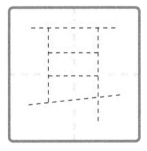
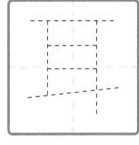
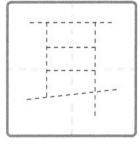
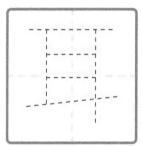
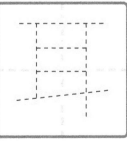
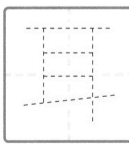
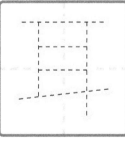
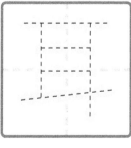

Character: 虫
English: worm
Strokes: 6
Pinyin: *chóng*

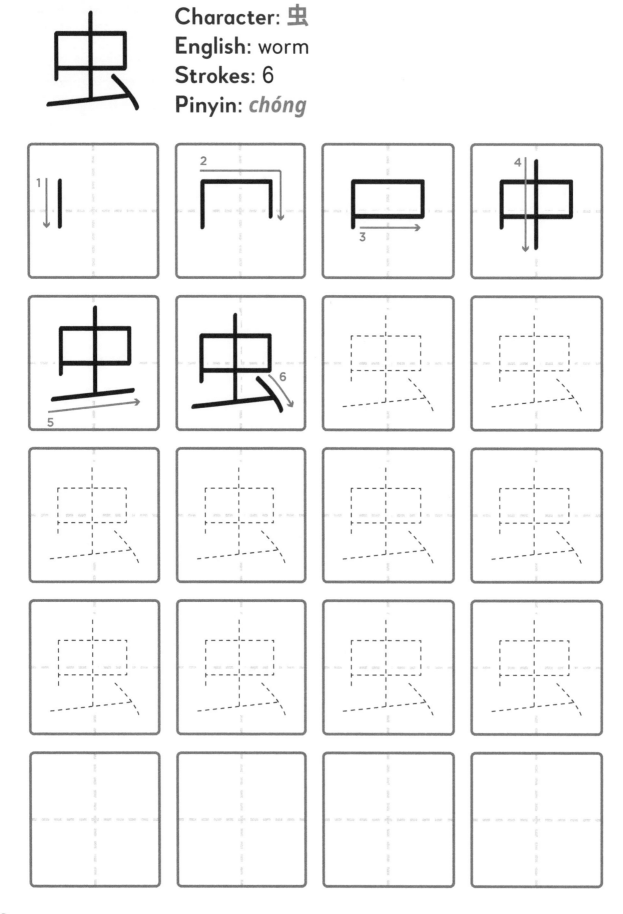

CHINESE CHARACTER PRACTICE WORKBOOK FOR KIDS

Character: 妈
English: mom
Strokes: 6
Pinyin: *mā*

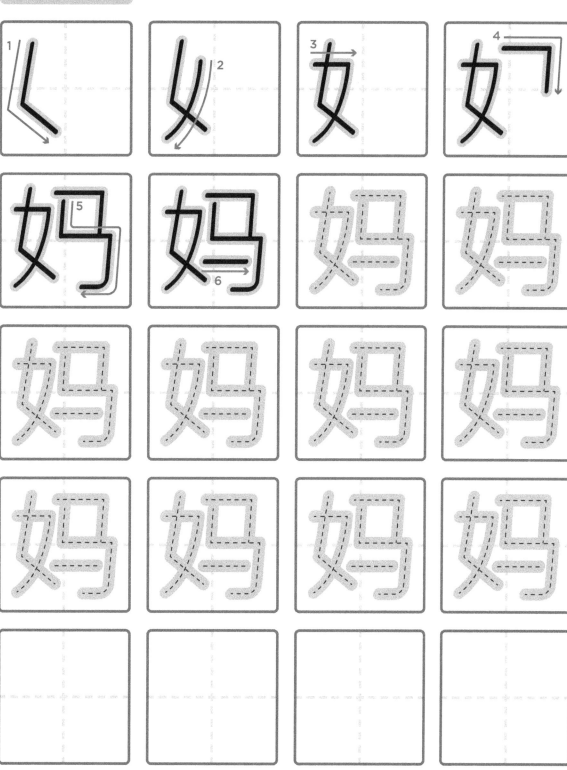

Character: 她
English: she/her
Strokes: 6
Pinyin: *tā*

 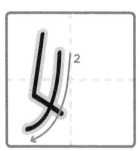  

  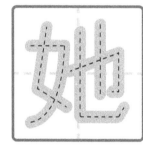 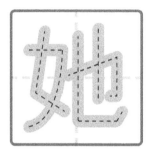

 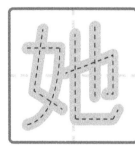 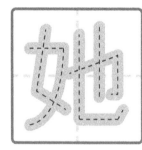 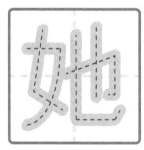

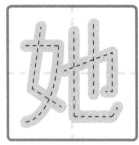 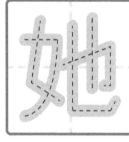 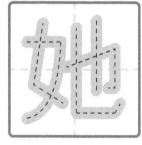 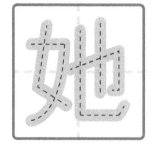

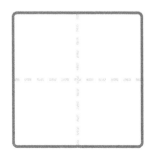  

Character: 关
English: close
Strokes: 6
Pinyin: *guān*

TIP
Write this character from top to bottom, starting with the two strokes at the top.

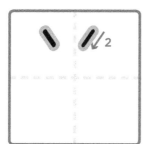

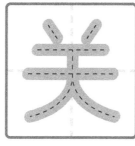

Character: 吃
English: eat
Strokes: 6
Pinyin: *chī*

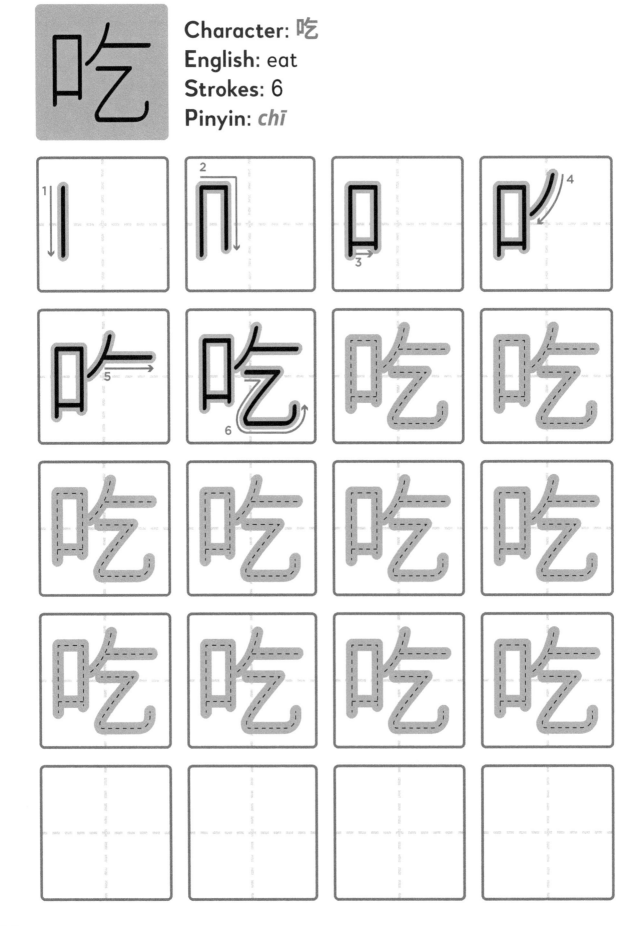

CHINESE CHARACTER PRACTICE WORKBOOK FOR KIDS

Character: 名
English: name
Strokes: 6
Pinyin: *míng*

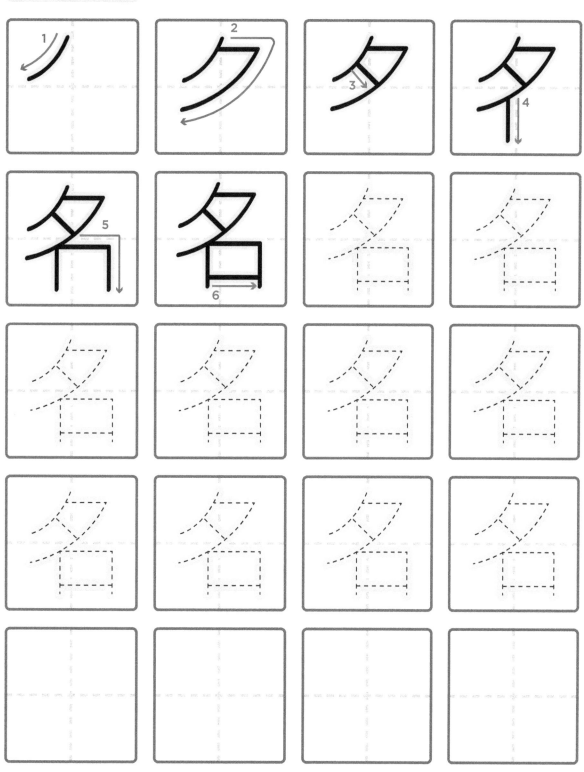

Character: 衣
English: clothes
Strokes: 6
Pinyin: *yī*

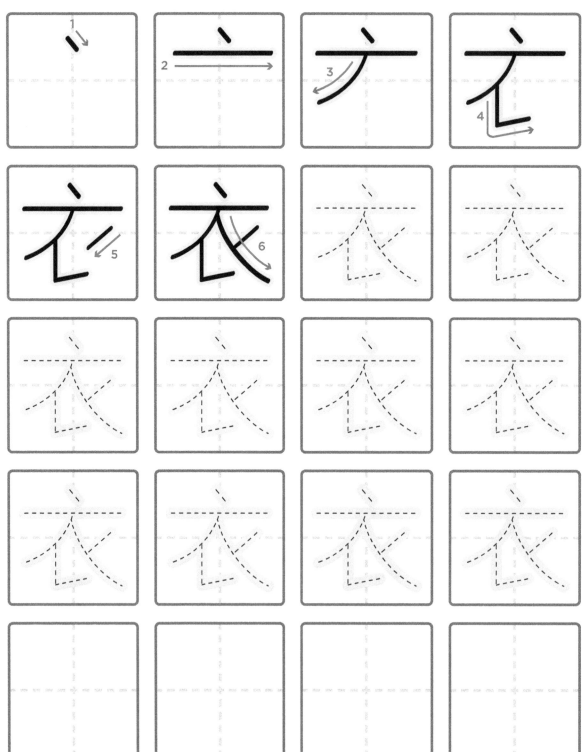

Character: 伞
English: umbrella
Strokes: 6
Pinyin: *sǎn*

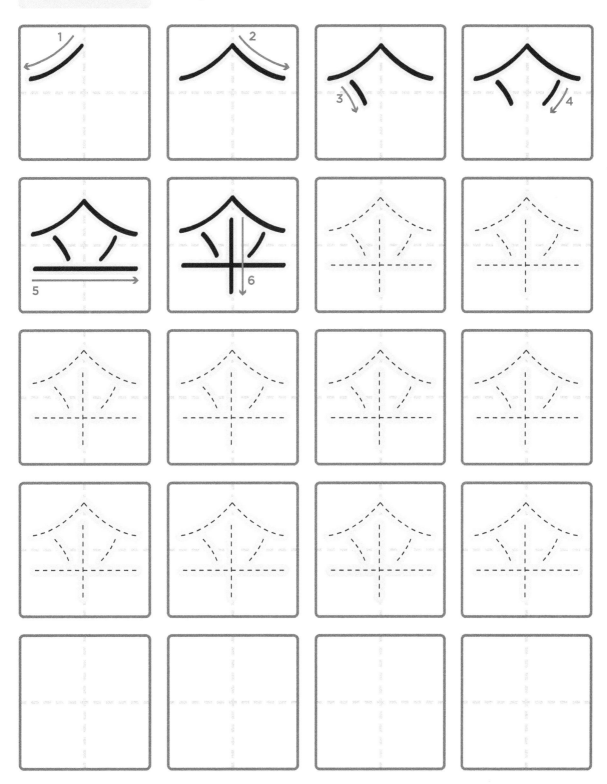

Character: 好
English: good
Strokes: 6
Pinyin: *hǎo*

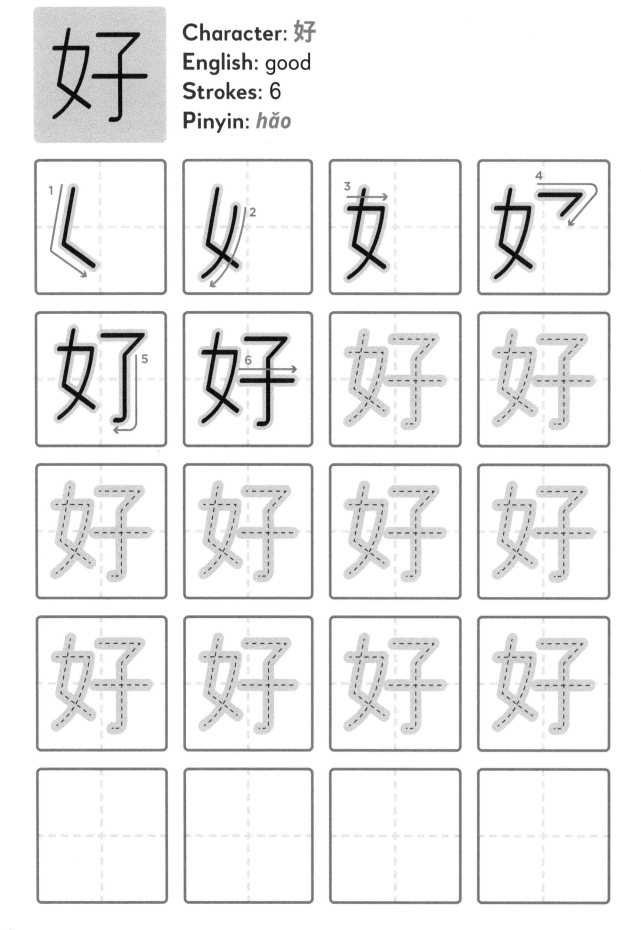

Character: 问
English: ask
Strokes: 6
Pinyin: *wèn*

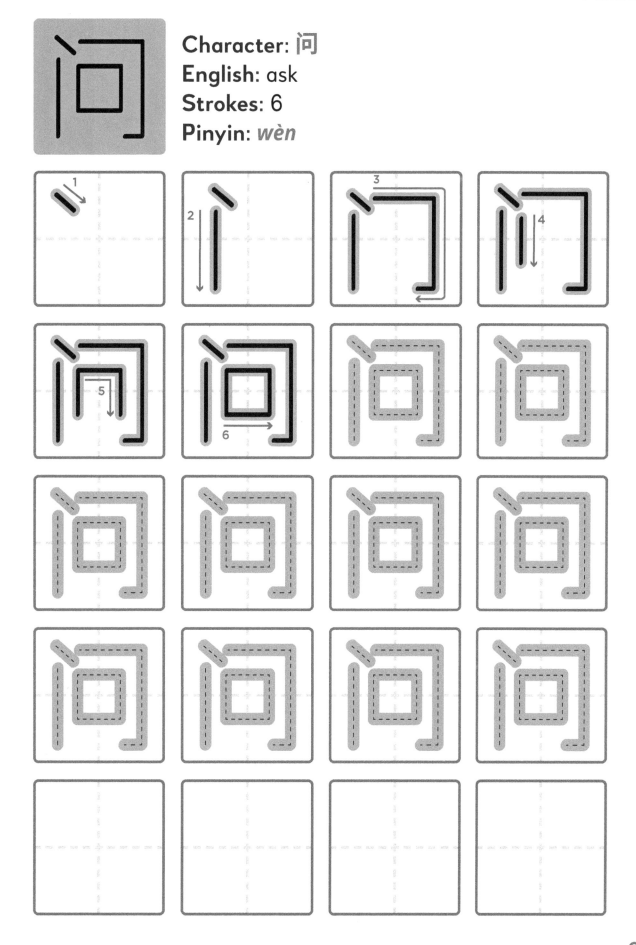

Character: 男
English: male/man
Strokes: 7
Pinyin: *nán*

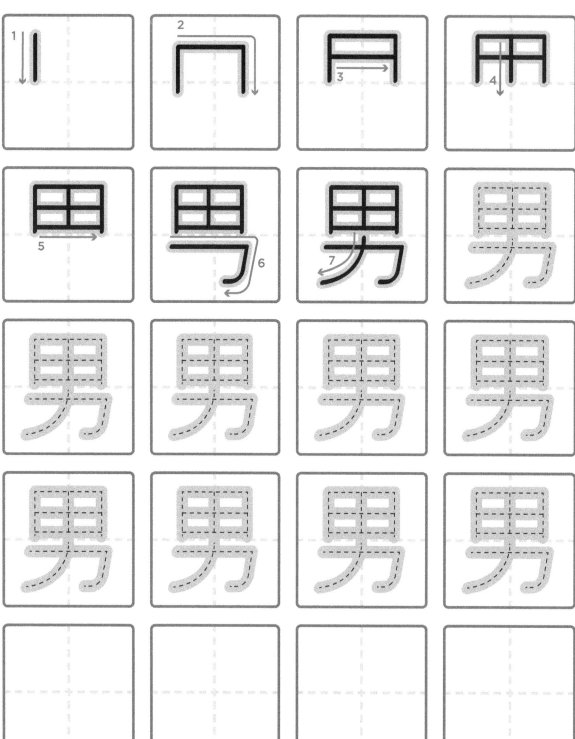

Character: 鸡
English: chicken
Strokes: 7
Pinyin: *jī*

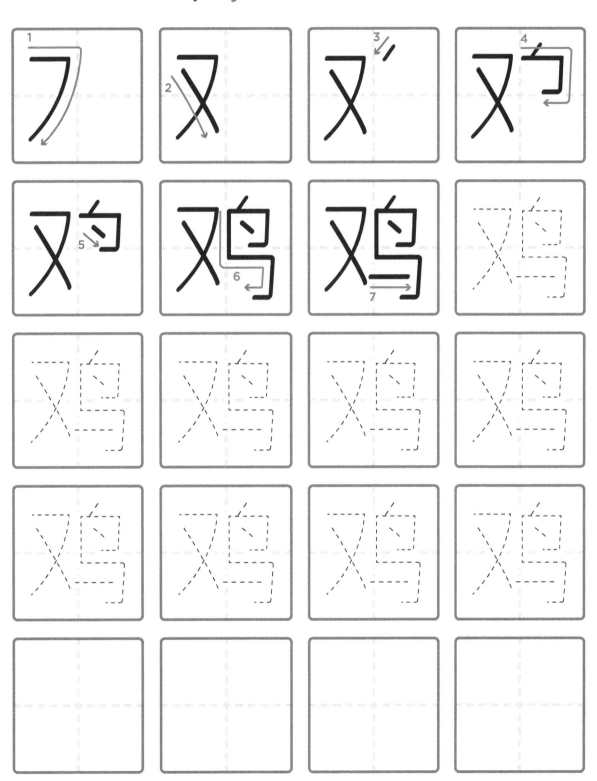

Character: 听
English: listen
Strokes: 7
Pinyin: *tīng*

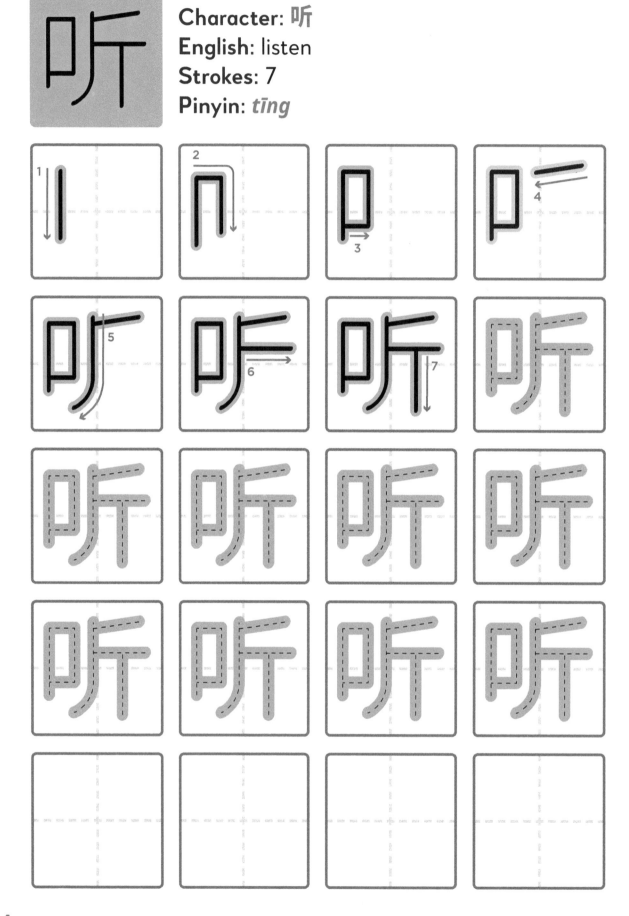

Character: 明
English: bright
Strokes: 8
Pinyin: *míng*

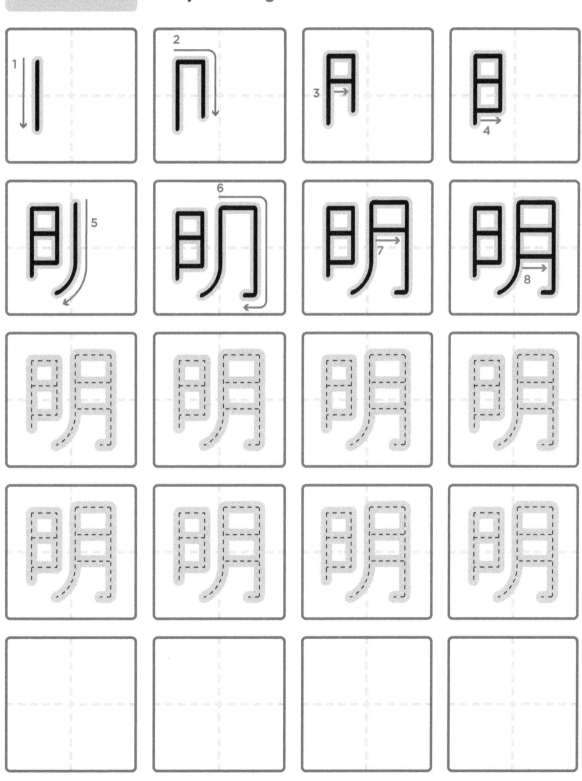

Character: 林
English: woods
Strokes: 8
Pinyin: *lín*

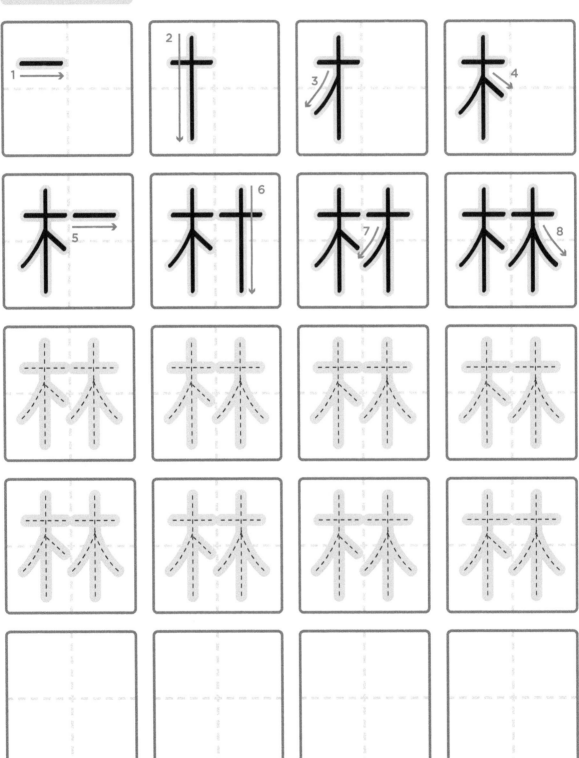

Character: 雨
English: rain
Strokes: 8
Pinyin: *yǔ*

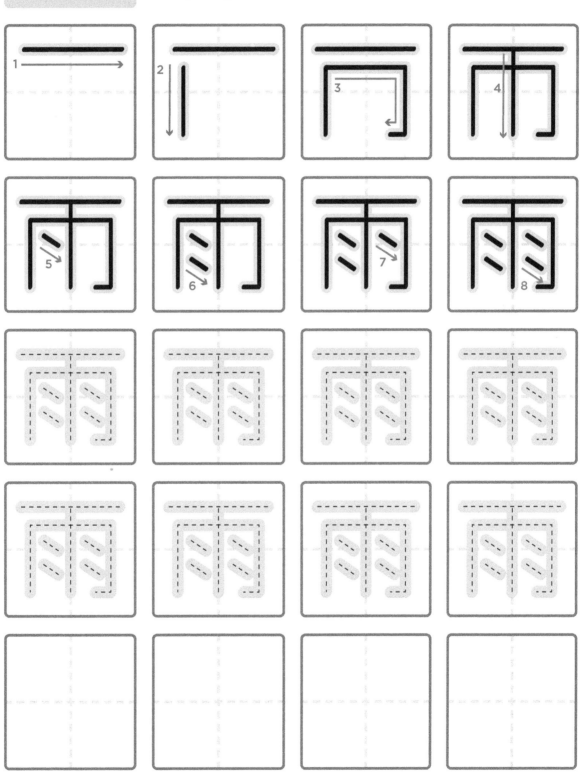

Character: 鱼
English: fish
Strokes: 8
Pinyin: *yú*

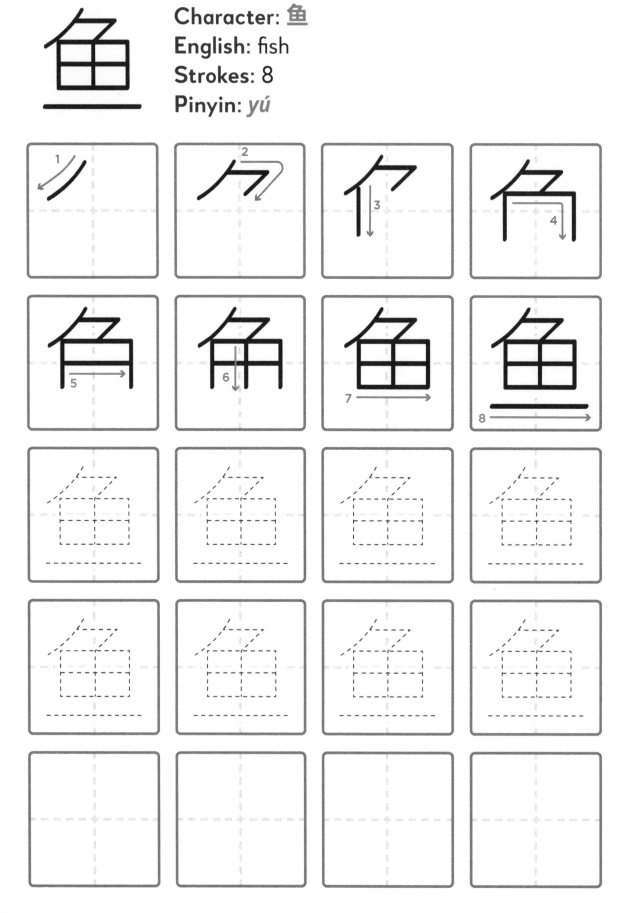

Character: 朋
English: friend
Strokes: 8
Pinyin: *péng*

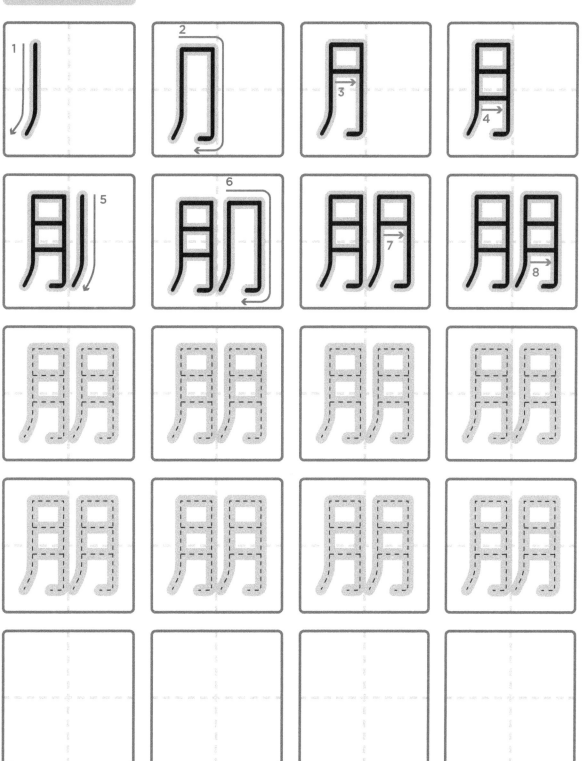

Character: 学
English: study/learn
Strokes: 8
Pinyin: *xué*

 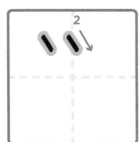 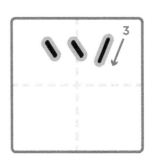 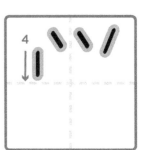

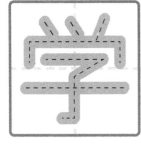   

  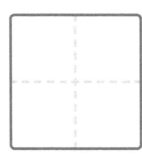 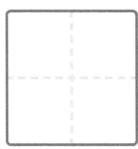

More Practice Space

The best way to make writing Chinese characters easy is to practice! Use these next pages to practice writing the characters we've explored in this book.

PRACTICE

MORE PRACTICE SPACE

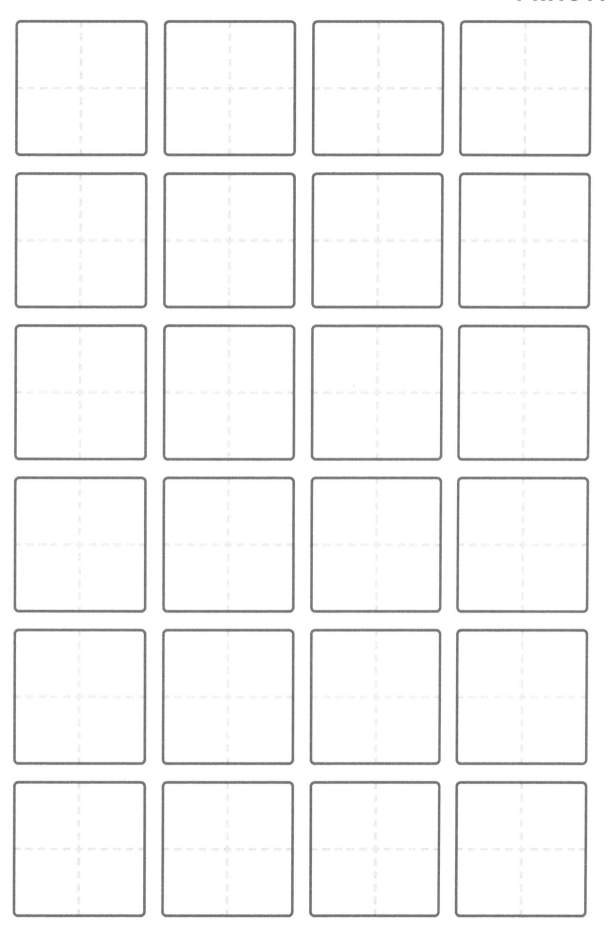

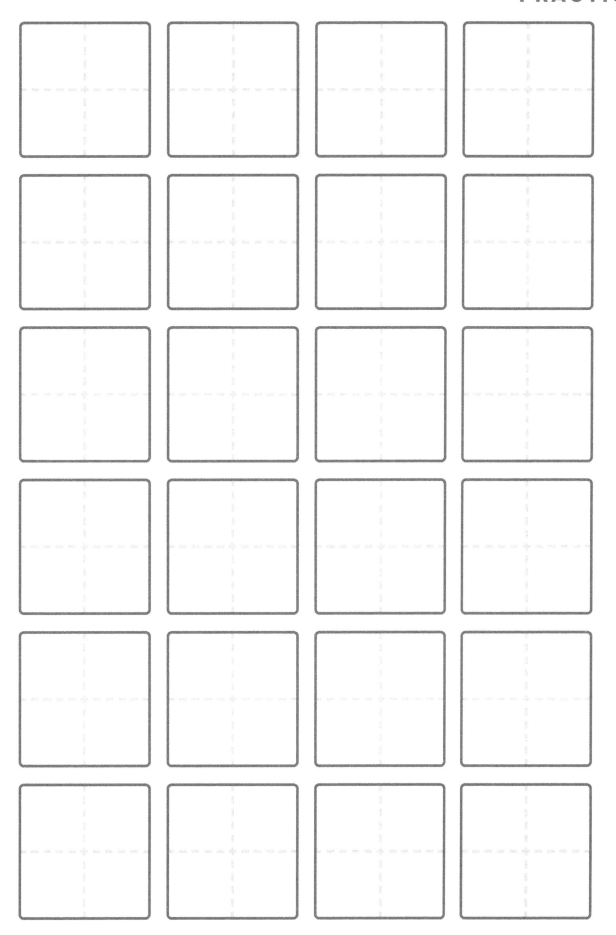

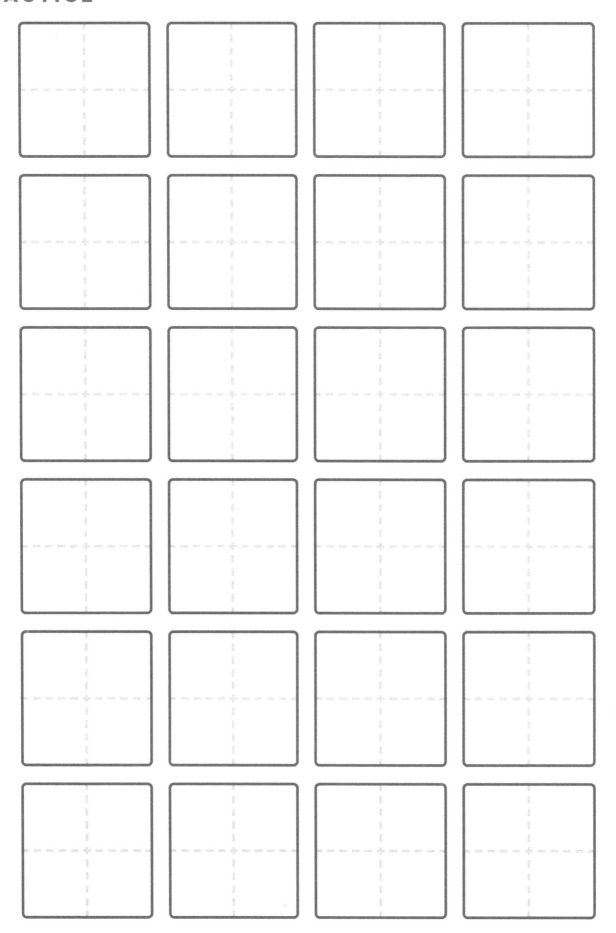

MORE PRACTICE SPACE

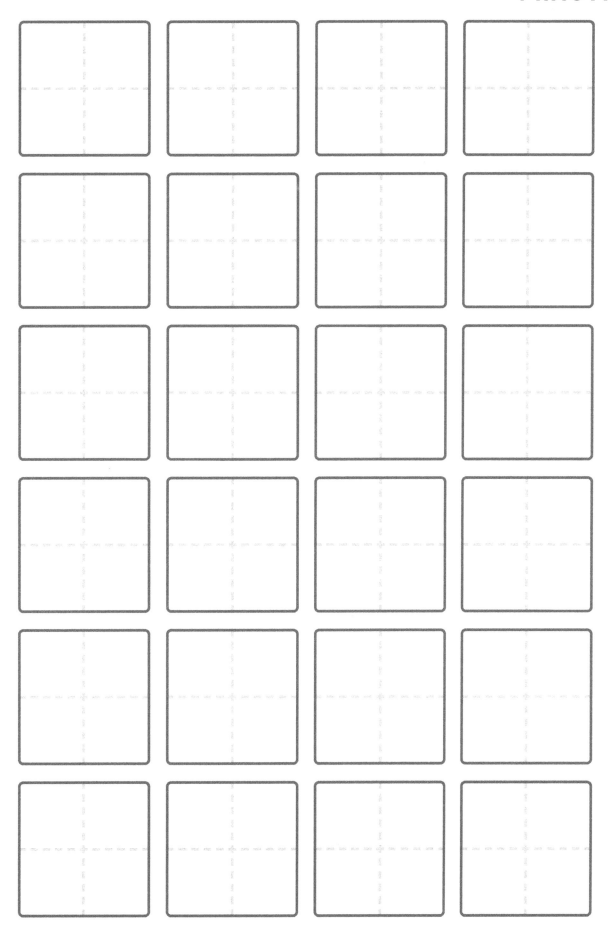

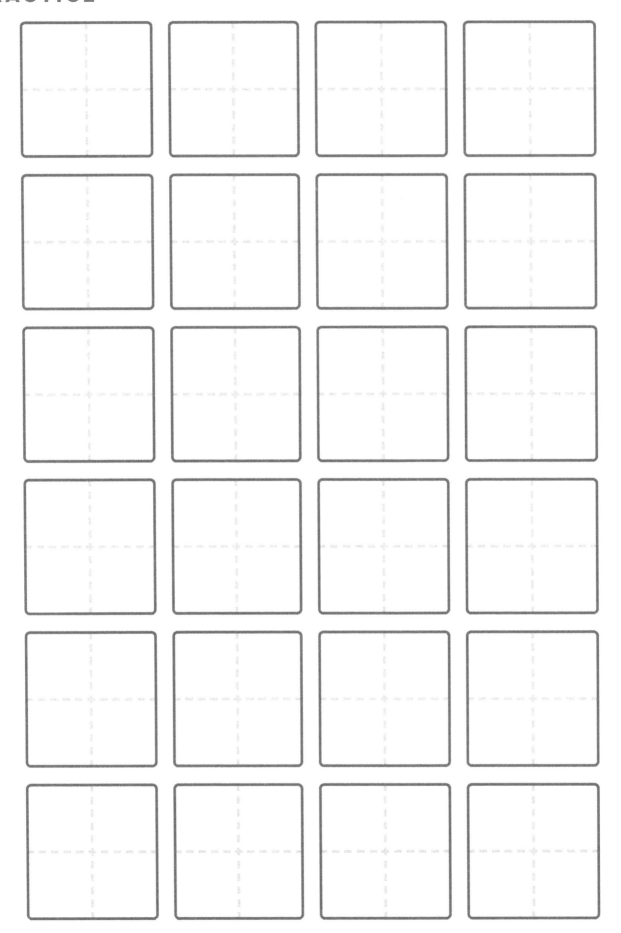

MORE PRACTICE SPACE

PRACTICE

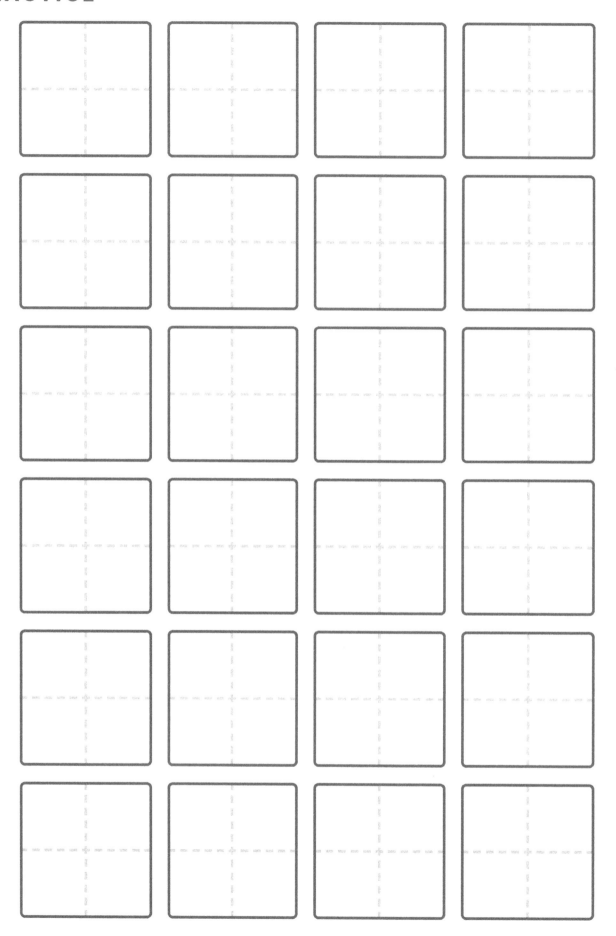

MORE PRACTICE SPACE

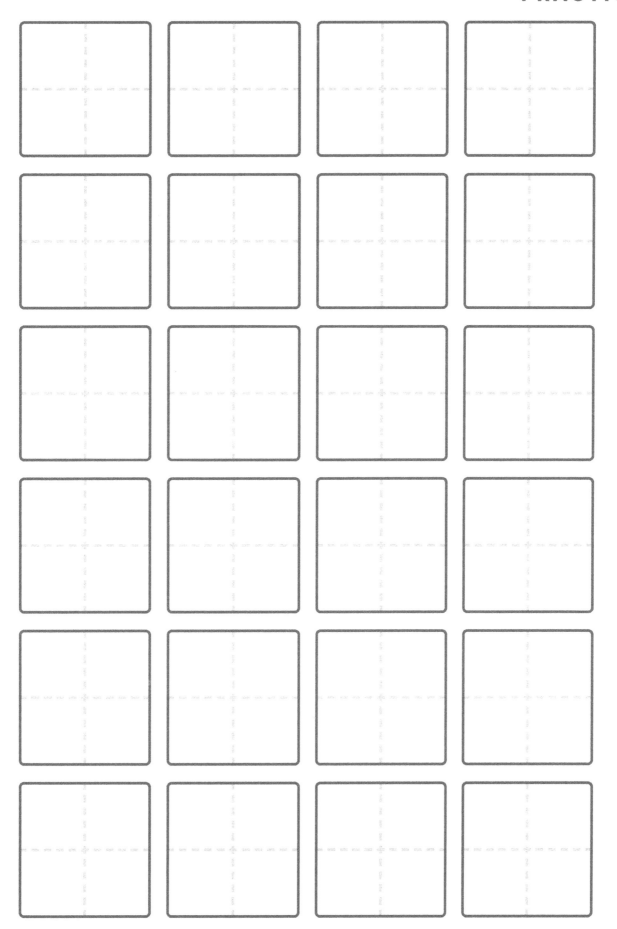

Common Chinese Phrases

你好！Hello!

他是我的朋友。He is my friend.

妈妈不喜欢吃鱼。Mom doesn't like to eat fish.

你喜欢什么颜色？What color do you like?

我喜欢红色。I like red.

下雨了。你有雨伞吗？It is raining. Do you have an umbrella?

我是学生。I am a student.

Resources

YOUTUBE CHANNELS
Chinese Buddy

Little Fox Chinese

WEBSITES/APPS
LittleChineseReaders.com

PandaTree.com

Pleco Chinese Dictionary

Skritter

PODCASTS
Popcorn Stories (故事爆米花)

MUSIC
Chinese Children's Classics v. 1.0 by A Little Mandarin

Let's Learn Mandarin Chinese with Miss Panda!
by Amanda Hsiung-Blodgett

Little Dragon Tales by Shanghai Restoration Project

About the Author

Rachel Avrick, MA, visited Asia while in college, working with a nonprofit and attending the prestigious University of Hong Kong. It was there that she fell in love with the Chinese language and culture. Returning to the United States, she completed her bachelor's degree in economics and Chinese with an Asian studies minor. She studied in Shanghai under the Critical Language Scholarship Program and taught in Taiwan for two years as a Princeton fellowship scholar. After living in Asia for five years, she returned to the United States, where she received her master's degree in curriculum and development. She now teaches Mandarin Chinese in the Chicago Public School system. She loves creating engaging materials for young Mandarin Chinese learners through her brand, Lessons with Laoshi.